3.a

Academic Standards and Expectations
The Role of EAP

Academic Standards and Expectations
The Role of EAP

Edited by Hilary Bool and Philip Luford

NOTTINGHAM
University Press

Nottingham University Press
Manor Farm, Main Street, Thrumpton
Nottingham, NG11 0AX, United Kingdom

NOTTINGHAM

First published 1999

British Library Cataloguing in Publication Data
Book Title: Standards and Expectations in the Academic Environment
I. Bool, Hilary II. Luford, Philip

ISBN 1-897676-69-7

Typeset by Nottingham University Press, Nottingham
Printed and bound by The Cromwell Press, Trowbridge, Wiltshire

Contents

Introduction

Hilary Bool and Philip Luford
University of Nottingham

As academic institutions throughout the English-speaking world are actively seeking to encourage enrolment by students from outside their shores, it would seem appropriate for there to be a greater awareness of the need for and the place of English for Academic Purposes (EAP) within tertiary education. An indicator that this is so is the increase in institutional and individual associate membership of the British Association of Lecturers in English for Academic Purposes (BALEAP) and by the steady growth in attendance at the Association's biennial conferences over the past decade.

At BALEAP's twelfth biennial conference, organised by the Centre for English Language Education at the University of Nottingham in 1995, these issues were explored under the title "Standards and Expectations in the Academic Environment: International students and the role of EAP." Presenters of papers and workshops adopted a variety of approaches in order to share with other EAP practitioners their particular focus and areas of interest in this field. Several sub-themes emerged including the place of EAP within different course structures, socio-cultural factors and their influence on both international students and academic staff, the relationship between EAP and different subject specialisms, ways of dealing with differing linguistic and discourse competences and the nature of EAP itself and the place of the EAP teacher within the institutional setting. For this volume the papers, representing a selection of those given, have been grouped into three broad sections: EAP and institutional issues, EAP and academic discourse and genre and EAP and classroom perspectives.

Section one focuses on a number of issues concerning institutional organisation and value systems and considers the role of EAP unit in relation to these. Thorp and Harris open the volume with an ethnographic study which attempts to gain some idea of the interaction between international students and their institutional environment. Working from the perspective of the students themselves, their findings are somewhat disturbing. In their study, international students often found themselves marginalised by academic staff who were not only insensitive to many of their needs but even occasionally predjudiced in their classroom practice. Gavriel continues this theme as she analyses staff-produced instructional and preparatory course material and highlights the inappropriacy of much of it for international students. Finding much of the material culturally loaded in favour of young, British, male students, replete with slang, in-jokes and idiolects unintelligible to students from other cultures, she concludes with a call for the "internationalisation" of the language produced by academic staff. Moving away from issues of language and culture, Fanning examines a recent organisational change in EAP, that of the increasing tendency for these courses to be integrated within degree programmes. He finds many advantages and some disadvantages in such developments entailing as they do a different use of class time, an increase in self-access learning and a need, echoed in Gray's paper in Section 3, for greater learner autonomy. In their paper, Blue and Archibald focus on changes in the international student body itself as they acknowledge the growing number of European students on EAP courses in Britain. In their view such "Europeanisation" challenges the academic-needs-directed nature of traditional EAP courses and may lead, in the future, to a restructuring of EAP provision in order to serve more effectively this group of students whose language requirements appear general rather than specific and whose motivation is often integrative rather than narrowly instrumental.

The second section groups together papers which consider the heterogeneity of discourse and genre in academic disciplines and the implications of this both for international students trying to become proficient performers within these contexts and for the EAP practitioners endeavouring to help them achieve this. The first two papers look at issues concerning the whole area of EAP. Lockett enters the debate about whether EAP should be narrowly subject-specific or more generalist by proposing the need for an informed focus on what he calls "general academic discourse." This he suggests can be drawn from a range of approaches such as genre analysis, rhetoric studies, the social construction of science, and more specifically, modes of linguistic signalling, the differing functions of academic discourse, and the way authors "hedge" truth claims in their writing. This could operate as an enabling resource for students within what he refers to as the "transitional pedagogy" of EAP. Turner calls into question the traditional conceptualisation of language within academic discourse, including EAP. Because, in her view, language is mistakenly seen as an invisible conduit for the expression of meaning, the competency problems of non-native speaking students are often seen as technical problems artificially isolated from the institutional and cultural matrix in which the production of academic English is embedded. The following papers in this section focus on particular skills or linguistic areas in their exploration of the varied nature of academic discourse and genres. Clarke and Saunders address the "double burden" of international students who must learn to operate, and, in particular to write, in multi-disciplinary, multi-genre, and cross-disciplinary environments and must do this, of course, in a second language. Imber and Parker consider an oral skills area they claim is often overlooked in EAP programmes yet is one in which international students need to acquire competence. For often they need to negotiate not only formal academic environments but those "blended" spoken discourses such as staff social functions and office chat that combine social and professional discourse registers. Badger argues that the teaching of discrete grammatical items cannot be divorced from the specific genre in which they occur. He offers some student-oriented techniques for understanding and describing grammar specific to Legal English. Finally in this section, Montemayor-Borsinger uses Theme Analysis to show that even within the highly restricted genre of the scientific research article a number of linguistic choices producing important rhetorical effects can be made.

Section three is more closely concerned with techniques and activities in the EAP classroom but nonetheless these examples of 'best' practice are firmly grounded in appropriate linguistic theory and analysis of student needs. Gray maintains that much teaching overlooks the diversity of student motivation, competencies and learning strategies in EAP. She believes that classes centred on learner autonomy and syllabus negotiation provide a way of integrating such diversity. Vincent continues this theme, arguing for a greater recognition of student experience as a teaching and learning resource. She looks at ways of combining peer support and shared learning techniques in the academic writing classroom. McDevitt considers the teaching of essay planning and referencing and claims that course book exercises are often too mechanical and artificial. Thornton addresses the problem of non-participation by international students in activities where speech is the medium. She maintains that linguistic competence is only one of several important reasons for this and suggests that group size, communication apprehension and the unconscious gender bias of some teachers are also factors to be taken into account. Montgomery and Pearsall study the differing assessment priorities of subject and EAP tutors and recommend the need for clearer guidelines for EAP tutors regarding departmental assessment priorities. Liu and Nesi, in a study which shows that international students may have a weaker grasp of technical vocabulary than traditionally thought, challenge the generally accepted notion that EAP should concentrate solely on the teaching of sub-technical vocabulary. In the final paper of the volume, Howarth, in an examination of collocations in academic writing, demonstrates that even native speakers have imperfect control over their use, a finding with obvious ramifications for the EAP classroom.

Taken as a whole these papers reveal not only an awareness among EAP practitioners of the need to verify what are often assumptions made regarding standards to be met and expectations held by both students and the academic staff who teach them but also, and more importantly, a willingness to undertake the research necessary to accomplish this. In addition, they show the growing body of knowledge and skill within the EAP profession for dealing with the complexity and multiplicity of academic discourses on the one hand, and, on the other, for assisting students to better operate within the academic maze.

A willingness to listen to the students in order to gain better understanding of their experiences and identify the difficulties they encounter clearly comes through in these papers. In investigating the question of standards and expectations within the academic environment, there is also recognition of the need for academic staff to be included in this communication process. Indeed, as many of these papers suggest, EAP may in one respect be viewed as a bridge between the international student and the institution. Many EAP teachers already work closely with their academic subject counterparts, perhaps a future conference could seek to take this collaboration further for the benefit of all within the academic community?

PART ONE:

EAP AND INSTITUTIONAL ISSUES

Language, Culture and Learning: Some Missing Dimensions to EAP

Roxy Harris[1] and Dilys Thorp[2]
[1]*School of ELT, Thames Valley University;* [2]*Freelance Consultant/Trainer*

INTRODUCTION AND PROCEDURE

This study was sponsored by the Ethnic and Cultural Diversity Enterprise in a Higher Education (HE) project to explore in more depth issues that had been raised earlier (e.g. Thorp 1991) about the effect on learning of different cultural expectations. The purpose of this stage of research was to try to view more closely, through the eyes of the students themselves, the total learning context for which EAP tries to provide support, especially in the light of the recent huge expansion in higher education which includes an increase in the numbers of part-time and mature students. We were therefore decided to pursue an ethnographic approach, involving participant observation and ethnographic interviews. This is in contrast to some previous and current work, for example Bird et al (1992), Grundy (1993) and Barge and McCarthy (1995), which had used questionnaires or group interviews, and started from a particular hypothesis or problem. We approached this study with relatively open minds and no overt agenda of our own, hoping to capture insights from the informants' standpoint that we felt more quantitative approaches denied. We had no predetermined questions. Rather, we wanted to so embed ourselves in the students' environment that, over time, key issues would emerge from our informants. As Hammersley and Atkinson (1983) explain:

> *The ethnographer participates, overtly or covertly, in people's daily lives for an extended period of time, watching what happens listening to what is said asking questions ... In fact collecting whatever data are available to throw light on the issues with which he/she is concerned.*

The eventual procedure we adopted was an ethnographic approach, but in a greatly reduced form. We were not able to embed ourselves as full time researchers since we continued with our full time teaching commitments, and the scale of our study was smaller than originally envisaged. We were not, for example, able to shadow students in multiple settings as originally planned, nor, with one exception, were we able to carry out ethnographic interviews with staff. Thus we were not able to obtain the triangulation originally planned. Clearly our work makes no attempt to be representative, but, as Evans (1988) says of his own qualitative studies: '*the validity ... does not depend on numbers but on [his] necessarily subjective efforts to understand the whole through close attention to individuals.*'

It is in this light that we offer the study.

The study involved first year a Higher National Diploma (HND) Hotel and Catering students at a large higher education institution. To set the work up we first attended a mass lecture of the whole year group to introduce ourselves and familiarise ourselves with one aspect of their course. We then each sat in on whatever classes our own teaching commitments allowed. The purpose of this was partly participant observation, partly to familiarise the students with us, and partly as a means of making contact with potential informants. This was our only contact with the students: the people who became our informants were those who made the most relaxed contacts with us in the course of our participation in their classes.

The method used by each of the two researchers here was slightly different: RH attended IT sessions and acted as an IT support tutor, since he was comfortable and skilled in an IT environment, whilst DT attended practical workshops in the kitchen and restaurant, in which she joined in alongside students practising skills such as silver service, and carrying heavy trays. This initial process of sitting in on classes lasted several weeks.

Once volunteers emerged, individual ethnographic interviews were arranged. Interviews took place at a mutually convenient time, and tended to last between one and one and a half hours, and were always held on either the student's ground (e.g. the refectory) or a neutral area such as an off-campus cafe, never in our offices. The interviews proceeded through open questions such as the following:

> What has stood out for you during the last week?
> What sort of day have you had?
> When you talk to your friends about the course, what do you say about it?
> When you look back over the year since September, what stands out?
> How's the course going?

In total we had almost 70 contacts with our informants either in interviews or in some of their learning contexts over a six month period.

Part of our technique was to recap on what had been said in previous interviews and get clarification or expansion on points made earlier, in order to probe issues raised by informants in more depth. Our informants all had more than one opportunity to talk about a particular issue, although this worked differently for the two researchers. While DT saw one of her informants on ten separate occasions, RH saw five informants, on their own, on average three times each. DT's interviews with ML in particular have the benefit of capturing her hindsight and reflection, rather than just transient feelings. In this way key issues came to be revealed over a series of interviews.

It is important to emphasise here that the study did not arise out of a 'problem syndrome', but took place in positive circumstances. The people who became our informants were not those with any particular grouse and were generally students who were successful on the course. In obtaining our informants we were not prescriptive in our view of ethnic and cultural diversity, and the significance of this approach will be evident from the descriptions of the informants in the next section.

BACKGROUND OF INFORMANTS

Informant ML ML is ethnically Chinese but was brought up and educated in London. Her parents are Hong Kong Chinese, and run a Chinese restaurant in London. She had already been to college before coming on this course as she had attended a Further Education (FE) college for two years doing 'A' levels. At twenty she was a couple of years older than some of her classmates who had come straight from school.

Informant JW A mature middle aged student of Jamaican background. She has a son/daughter now living away from home.

Informant SJ Male, white, aged 24. British born and brought up in a middle class milieu. Italian/Sicilian background on one side of his family, English on the other. He said that culturally he feels 80% Italian. Languages include English, Italian and Spanish.

Informant DD Female, white, aged 33. Irish born and brought up and Irish schooling . She had lived in Algeria for 10 years. She has a teenage son. Languages include English and Arabic.

Informant CG Female, black, aged about 20/21, African. Born in Uganda. Lived in Kenya from age 8 to 16. She came to the U.K. at the age of 16. Languages include Madi (Ugandan language), English and Swahili.

Informant HP Female, black, aged 23, African. Born and brought up in Zimbabwe. In Britain for 2 years. Languages include Shona (Zimbabwean language) and English.

Informant RA White, male, aged 23, Italian/Sicilian. After leaving compulsory schooling at the age of 14, he had studied at catering school for 5 years leaving with a diploma. He had been in Britain, on and off, for about 3 years. Languages include Italian, Sicilian, English and German.

There is a description, above, of the process by which the informants were selected. However, very often research of this kind which attempts to analyse differing student perceptions of their learning tends to construct essentialised student groups under headings such as "overseas students" or "ethnic minority students". The student informants in this study confound such categorisations. Although only one of the seven informants was British-born, none of them fitted into the category of "overseas students" in its traditional meaning of someone newly arrived in Britain and with extremely limited knowledge of the British context.

Informants SJ, DD and RA were white but with English, Italian/Sicilian and Irish ethnicity. Informant DD had also a long experience of an Arabic culture and a son whose father was an Algerian. Informants CG and HP, though born and brought up in Africa, had both had several years of experience of living and working in Britain. Informant ML, while being ethnically Chinese, had spent most of her life in Britain. Finally, informant JW, while born in Jamaica, had long years of experience of living and working in Britain, and bringing up a family here. All the informants were extremely well acquainted with English either as a mother tongue or as an additional language acquired to a high level of competence.

In sum, then, if the minefield of suggesting cultural differences in perceptions of learning experiences in higher education is going to be entered, it must be on the basis of a much more complex picture of what cultural difference might mean. For instance in this study, sometimes the informants' perceptions were governed by cultural experiences mediated by age. At other times racial factors seemed to be the key ones; while in other situations perceptions of ethnicity appeared to be determining points. It seems to us that future studies should attempt to look at students' perceptions not only along axes of social class, gender, race and ethnicity but in terms of complex combinations of these factors as they manifest themselves in individual students. This implies, too, that the notion of "British Culture", with which the culture of 'overseas' students is often contrasted, must be much more rigorously interrogated. We would argue that our informants in their culturally hybrid make up are not atypical or freakish but highly representative of the body of students in any educational institution in London. Hall (1988) has been explicit in his formulation on this point when he suggests that we are living through a period when the term 'ethnicity' is being contested and in which there:

> *is the splitting of the notion of ethnicity between, on the one hand the dominant notion which connects it to nation and 'race' and on the other hand what I think is the beginning of a positive conception of the ethnicity of the margins of the periphery. That is to say, a recognition that we all speak from a particular place, out of a particular history, out of a particular experience, a particular culture ...*

What was interesting in the present study was not the familiar insider/outsider binary constructed around notions of the overseas student / native British student, but the extent to which our informants perceived themselves as on the periphery, as outsiders at particular moments based on the earlier mentioned complex and shifting combination of factors connected with 'race', gender, class, age, language, culture and history. Indeed, as can be seen from the brief description of informants given above, the overseas student / native British student frame of analysis was disrupted by alternative frames which include, as a minimum, the following overgeneralised and rather crude ones: white British ethnicities; English-speaking ethnicities not based on being British or British ethnicities not based on being white; ethnicities wholly formed 'overseas;' ethnicities founded on a combination of both substantial British *and* substantial 'overseas' experience.

FINDINGS

Academic factors

Our concern to simply discover students' perceptions of what was going on, and to let them 'set the agenda', led to the emergence of a number of issues that we could not have anticipated. Early on we realised that what one might call 'narrow EAP factors' had important other dimensions to them, in particular the affective and the cultural. These factors intertwined with the more traditional skills areas of EAP to suggest a much more complex picture: that EAP cannot be seen as a set of technical skills in isolation, but rather is a melange of language, culture and affect. We shall discuss lectures and seminars as (academic) areas to illustrate this.

We would suggest that one weakness in considerations of EAP tends to be a concentration on the technicalities of how to assist students to achieve proficiency in EAP alone. What is neglected in this approach is a deep enough understanding of the total surrounding context within which students have to deploy English for Academic Purposes. This context includes general societal attitudes in Britain towards racial, ethnic and linguistic minorities, which are likely to be reflected in fellow students and lecturers. After all there is evidence of discrimination against ethnic minority students even at the point of entry to British universities (Connolly 1994 in Haselgrove (ed.))

One informant, SJ, with a white British background, spoke with feeling about an incident which arose in the context of a lecture and may well have occurred because of the frustration and inadequacy felt by a lecturer when confronted by the reality of the difficulties which the lecture format can cause for students struggling with English for Academic Purposes: A student of African background had not understood something the lecturer had said for language reasons connected with the speed of the lecturer's delivery and asked whether the lecturer could repeat the passage more slowly. The lecturer had pounced on her asking her whether she was stupid for not understanding what had been said.**[SJ]** The same informant found that there were language-related problems too for white European students.

> *A Danish girl couldn't answer one of the questions on the hygiene certificate exam which has to be passed to work in industry because she didn't know the English word and she felt too scared to go to the lecturer afterwards and say I'm sorry I don't know this word - rodent or something - she felt too embarrassed to ask the lecturer afterwards.* **[SJ]**

The point here is not whether or not the student is correct in feeling that she would get an unsympathetic hearing from her lecturer. It is, rather, that there is something more general in the atmosphere in the learning context which causes her to have this apprehension. What is interesting about SJ's comments is that he appears to make a direct linkage between incidents which could present themselves as purely EAP issues and general problems in the wider University context. As he saw it, not enough thought was given to the needs of students from overseas and ethnic minority students; there were many things that could be done, from extending the range of food on offer in the refectory, to considering how the student bar and general student union services could more genuinely reflect the ethnic and cultural diversity of the student body. He suggested, ironically, that as lecturers were fond of mentioning that foreign students were important to the University in revenue terms, more attention should be devoted to looking after them:

> *There should be more respect and sensitivity shown to foreign students - since lecturers claim they keep the college afloat ... the treatment of overseas students seems abrupt - the language side in lectures, seminars, written work.* **[SJ]**

In addition to the above questions it was also clear that lectures presented particular technical problems for students in this study for whom English is not the first and most natural language. This is not really so surprising considering the complex combination of skills required of them. Often they need to be able to simultaneously listen to, read and take notes in, the medium of English:

> *The problem with the lectures they put something on the OHP you've got to write down what is there plus in the meantime you've got to listen what they are talking about and that means personally I cannot do two things especially in another language as well.* **[RA]**

This informant managed to articulate a partial solution to his own problem:

> *There are many solutions. One I thought was to give previous handouts about what is going to be done in the lectures. You're going to read that as a student and you'll know what it's about. The teacher comes in and is going to explain that so it's not really new for you and in that case what happens because you've read it before and because the teacher is explaining you may see there are some points you didn't really understand and I think you can really catch them in your mind what you didn't understand, while the teacher is explaining and in the seminar group you can use it by asking questions.* **[RA]**

Further associated problems arose for students in this study who were offered seminars linked with the lectures they had attended. Informants thought the seminars were a useful part of the learning process in that they provided an opportunity to talk directly to lecturers and to ask questions in order to clarify specific points. Nevertheless, there were clearly students who, while badly needing to make use of the seminars, failed to do so:

> *We don't ask questions that much. Unless you understand something fully you're not going to turn round and ask questions about it, because you don't know what to ask.* **[CG]**

Indeed, making a link with the earlier point about the difficulties faced in lectures by students whose first language is not English, one informant said that his own notes taken down during lectures were not good enough. They certainly did not form a good enough basis on which to ask questions in a seminar.

The detailed interviews with ML shed further light on the intense pressures surrounding the pace of lectures including the use of acetates, and asking questions for students for whom English was not a first language. ML herself disliked *'copying down so much that I can't listen and absorb so I've no idea about it at the end,'* and commented that sometimes when she looked back over her notes after attending a lecture: *'it seems so unfamiliar that I can't remember ever having been in it.'*

It was, we were told, for this reason that some students: '*are skipping lectures 'cos it's easier to just copy someone's notes afterwards than sitting there struggling to listen and write*'.

Informant ML clearly had a pivotal role for her 'overseas' friends, whose dependence on her she was well aware of and concerned about: '*a lot of my overseas friends they always borrow my notes ... I wanna tell them they have to listen as well `cos they're all relying on my notes... what happens if one day I wasn't there? If I didn't turn up then who would they rely on?'*

Clearly the overseas students were finding their own survival strategies to cope with the varying styles of lecturers, the easiest of which was relying on ML. Our informants had clear ideas as to what was good and poor lecturing practice: *'if the lecturers had more overheads... (it would be easier) ... some of them just er talk in the lecture for the whole 50 minutes.'*

The problem of the pace of lectures and understanding the main points was exacerbated by additional problems in asking questions. In EAP teaching there is often the assumption of an ideal context for asking questions, but our study highlighted that this was often very far from being the case. On many occasions it proved extremely difficult for students to ask questions even if an opportunity was provided by the lecturer during a lecture or at the end, for a number of different reasons. Firstly, students felt they could not ask questions unless they had followed most of the lecture. If there was something they did not understand during the lecture they were likely to lose track and be unable to follow the rest of it; then at the end, if offered a chance to ask questions, they felt they had not understood enough to be able to do so. We have seen earlier that this applied even when follow-up seminars were offered precisely to provide students with an opportunity to deepen their understanding of the lecture content.

Another type of problem came from the impatience of other students and makes highly relevant the anxieties felt by certain of our informants concerning how they thought they might be perceived by British students and lecturers for whom English was a first language. According to ML, often when someone did ask a question at the end of a lecture, no-one was listening, '*everyone is rustling papers, fidgeting.*'

Effectively our informant was prevented from asking a question or of hearing any answer that might be forthcoming and this in turn acted as a disincentive to others considering asking questions. To insist on asking questions and receiving answers under these conditions would involve an immense act of self-assertion, particularly for students whose first language is not English. In fact, according to ML, the reality that '*everyone is restless and keen to get off*' was the reason why *'Lecturer A said there's no time for questions.*'

It is, then, too simplistic to think that the task of the EAP tutor is simply to help students with their academic writing skills and the language work involved in formulating questions, learning to interrupt and to ask for clarification. The onus was perceived by our informants as always being on ***students*** to ask questions of the lecturers, rather than the lecturers facilitating this in any way. In an environment like this in which the students perceive that neither lecturers nor other students welcome questions, they are unlikely to feel they can ask anyone other than a close friend who may well be equally in the dark. The cumulative effect of this contributes to their feeling peripheral and demonstrates one of the ways in which problems surrounding EAP can be masked rather than overtly revealed. The majority of our informants were people who did not have difficulties with English, and it was through them that we happened to find out about other students who were struggling - e.g. our British/ Hong Kong Chinese informant tended to mix with other ethnically Chinese students, and her concern about their problems emerged through an unravelling process of her talk and reflection in the ethnographic interviews.

Interaction

Our study showed that different cultural expectations amongst students and staff about such aspects as roles, social distance, duties, rights and obligations seriously affected students' learning. Interaction in student/staff relations impinged on learning in ways that we illustrate below. We suggest that this too is an area that is insufficiently addressed in EAP.

A. Student-staff relations [1]

There was clearly a mismatch between the way in which our informants viewed the role of academic staff and the apparent perceptions of staff. Mismatches of expectations have been discussed elsewhere in general terms, see for example Archer (1986) and Cortazzi (1990).

[1] Due to pressure of space we have not included the area of student-student interaction in this paper

Our data offers specific illustration of this and tries to move away from suggesting that specific ethnic groups can be said to behave in specific and homogenous ways.

Whilst our data highlights the complexity of the learning context, it shows, on the other hand, that our informants had highly specific expectations about appropriate behaviour from staff and students in each learning context. For example, what may have been a lecturer's way of expressing solidarity and co-membership with students could be perceived rather differently by specific individual students, as can be shown by the following extracts from the present study:

BHS, a mature student, said she disliked the way a particular lecturer *'fools around'* and *'the language he uses (fuck - you fucked it up)'*. She disapproved of the way the class were allowed to *'muck around'* when the lecturer *'then found it difficult to clamp down later.'* She also commented that *'staff should not be sitting around smoking with students at the end of the session'*.

ML, too, was definitely unimpressed by what she perceived as a lecturer's lightweight approach to a practical demonstration. This had *'been a flop'* as he had omitted an important ingredient, but then just joked about it afterwards. This student felt that they had missed out on seeing how to do it correctly, and felt uneasy about the joking.

Both these informants rationalised their unease. BHS suggested that maybe she herself was *'perhaps rather old fashioned... he (the lecturer) is so young'* whilst ML reflected that the lecturer's behaviour might be *'because he's from industry and he's not used to dealing with students.'*

On the other hand, ML was extremely happy when praised by staff, whether individually or as a member of a group. She commented with feeling that *'he* [a lecturer] *said oh you deserve to have some today cos you've worked very hard'* and before we left he just said '*Oh well done boys and girls*' and he said '*it was a very enjoyable session yesterday.*' Whilst the use of *'boys and girls'* seems condescending/patronising to the present authors, ML confirmed that she did not at all mind being addressed in this way. What counted was the praise. We see here the expectation of a different sort of staff-student relationship; evidence of student dependence on the teacher that may conflict with the institution's idea of the student as a self directed autonomous learner. We recognise that there are very many different styles of teaching and learning, and hesitate to make judgements about their merits and demerits. However, we suggest that the cumulative effect on our informants of instances of mismatch such as described above contributes to their feeling of being outsiders.

Three other important aspects of staff-student interaction emerged from the interviews with ML. These were issues surrounding the use of humour and jokes, the return of assignments, and knowledge of students' names. These themes were repeatedly returned to by this informant on many different occasions, and seemed to be key instances of ways in which she was often positioned as a troublesome outsider struggling to understand a milieu within which she was working. Although she was brought up in Britain and had no problems with the English language, she in many ways identified herself with the 'classic EAP overseas students'

1. Humour and jokes

Humour and jokes came up in several interviews with ML. She commented that some of the jokes made by one lecturer were *'really insulting'*. Lecturers may well have made jokes in an attempt to show friendship and solidarity with their students, or to lighten the atmosphere

- and indeed, according to our informants they succeeded in getting laughs from the younger students whom our informants identified as 'white British school leavers.' But for other students such as ML these jokes took place in a different context. One of several such examples occurred when a lecturer attempted to make a joke concerning her family's Chinese restaurant.

> *He said, 'I was going to go to your restaurant on Friday ML', and then I asked him 'why didn't you?' and then he goes 'because I went to a better one'. He laughed and everyone else laughed too.*

This exchange took place in the context of this lecturer's previous remarks about the 'tacky' nature of Chinese restaurants, and his regular use of Chinese restaurants as examples of bad practice. It also takes place in the general historical context in Britain in which disparaging remarks have routinely been made about Chinese restaurants. From ML's point of view it was like *: 'being back at primary school ... all these racist jokes ... I always have racist jokes made about me because I'm the only Chinese, I look different etc.'*

2. Return of assignments

The return of assignments was an issue frequently talked about by ML and it had a clear interactional dimension. Firstly, she said that several of her group could not understand why it took so long to have their assignments returned to them, especially when they knew they had already been marked. Work was still not being returned, she said, despite their repeated attempts to retrieve it. This problem had a direct bearing on learning, in that without the return of a marked piece of work students felt they couldn't learn from their weaknesses and mistakes before producing the next assignment. But there was also an indirect effect, accruing from the interactional problems around this. The issue became very serious to ML, who commented that after many attempts by the group to get their work returned, the member of staff concerned had been *'unpleasant ... to all of us'*; students had, she said, *'been fobbed off'* and *'shouted at'* when asking for the work, and because of this were at a loss as to how to ever get it back. A similar problem arose with another member of staff, and this became for ML the very serious issue of a particular lecturer not keeping a promise:

> *she promised (to return ML's and other students' work) that's what she promised one day when I went to see her and she goes 'all right I'll put them all in the Faculty Office and you can go and collect them on Tuesday afternoon' ... there were no assignments there ... nor anything.*
>
> *... the lecturers as well they're all saying they're really busy but we just want our assignments back. It won't take 30 seconds ... you can just like dump the whole pile on the floor or whatever and we will sort them out ourselves ... I don't know if they do keep them in a big safety lock or something and it takes them hours to pick the lock ... I don't know what's the problem all we just want is just to have it back ... well she knew that I'd passed she says oh you are so and so and I goes yes and you passed then I said 'yes' (she said) 'cos oh thank God for that so you don't need to see me...*
>
> *... so that means when I pass I don't have to go and see her and discuss about having to do the assignment again. So she says 'Oh thank God for that you*

passed so what you can do is come back to me on Monday and then she goes come and see her on Monday ... I went to see her on Monday she said she was busy so I had to collect it from the Faculty Office the next day and they still haven't got it.

For conscientious students like ML this issue of the return of assignments was a prime example where there appeared to be a substantial and obviously distressing misunderstanding between students and staff about their respective responsibilities, rights and duties.

3. Names

Towards the end of the interviews with ML an issue emerged which had been highly significant for her and many of her fellow students throughout the academic year. This was the question of how staff handled students' names. It is interesting to reflect that it emerged only towards the end of the year, perhaps because it was only then that ML felt able to trust the interviewer, DT, enough to talk about something as negative as this. ML complained that even her own tutor still, in May, after eight months, did not know how to read out her name although she had specifically explained it to him. The following comments show that this member of staff had similar problems with a number of other Chinese names, and we see again how pivotal this informant, ML became for a section of those perceived as 'overseas' students.

It took him a very long time to get to know ... to know my name he didn't know what to call me he called me Miss Lau and then he called me Li Ling or he just called me Miss Miss and things like that and he couldn't get my name right ... he still doesn't know which order it comes in and I said to him 'My surname is Lau and my first names are Mei Li but I like to be called Li' and it was really funny yesterday in the lecture he was going through the whole of the HND first year the names in the lecture theatre yesterday it was just in case if anybody's missed out cos he needs the full list for the final exam grades and when he reached my name he goes 'Er we've got a Lau Li Mei or whatever it is' ... And it's written ... with the surname first Lau and it I want to say to him just read it off the paper ... it says Lau and then Mei Li. And he just says ' Well we've got a Lau Li Mei or whoever whatever it is, he's still I was really ... still he's taught me for a whole year now and he still doesn't know my name. He's my tutor as well, and I've tried explaining to him that Lau is my surname and Mei Li are my two Christian names but 1 like to be called Li ... and he doesn't it just doesn't click to him ...

... all the Oriental names he had a lot of trouble saying my friend's name was erm, he goes 'Is this right? H- O-N-G Hong Hung and whatever it is' and everyone started laughing ... and then ... I've got a friend called Hai Si Ho and he said Hi De Hi, Hi De Ho and everyone was laughing ... and you know Ping Kai? He goes, he says 'Ping Pong' and her surname's W-o-n-g which is pronounced Wong ...

This informant noted a stark contrast between this lecturer's behaviour here and when he was reading out names which he clearly perceived as unproblematically 'British':

Dawson ... he said it no problems ... all these names and then when he got to us he just ... Whereas it was like Susan Wilson, Sophie Butcher, Stephen Scott-Jacobson, Stuart ... started stuttering and can't he just read it off the paper?

[In order to protect our informants these names have been changed after consultation with a Chinese speaker, and every effort has been made to select equivalent alternatives in order to retain the flavour of the original quotations]

Fundamental to how students feel themselves positioned is the question of how they are addressed. We would suggest that if the student receives the implied message that they have a 'difficult' name, not worth bothering about or unusual, this places that student as an outsider. Staff inability to correctly handle 'foreign' student names would seem to affect students' perceptions of how they are seen by staff, and the extent to which they feel alien from or part of the group.

B. Student - institution interaction

1. Practical assessment

One area of difficulty which emerged was the question of practical assessment. In this study the system of assessing restaurant practice on their course aroused disquiet amongst several of the informants, partly because they were not clear about the basis on which it was carried out and partly because they suspected that the system might not be fair. More disturbingly, it was clear from the informants that considerable discussion had taken place amongst the students speculating on whether variations in their grades in the restaurant assessment had a racial or cultural bias. The force of this feeling was even more compelling given that one of the informants who spoke most passionately on the issue had in fact attained a high grade in this assessment:

It still goes on like in the restaurant we thought it would change. Last week er in the past 2 weeks soon after the holiday we were having our Competence Test for ... restaurant service. I think. I mean if you notice if you look at the results all the black people we were lower than all the white people even those who never used to come to college or work they still got higher marks than us. I mean when I start comparing with anybody else I'm much better than anybody else but still they give you a lower mark ...

... all the white people were ranging from 87% to 80 from 82% to 87% and I was the first one to get 81 ... but the white people made a lot of mistakes, a lot of mistakes all over the place but still they get higher marks you don't know why than the other students but it just happens.

Yeah of course. I don't feel happy of course. We still have a chance to talk to the teachers and ask them why did you give me 81%. I deserve something better cos I don't know I ... looking at myself looking at what they were they were looking at ... I don't feel and I still don't know why I went wrong ... when we are talking about it as students we ... as if because we are black but

> *we'll never know maybe we're not too sure we're not, we're not, we're not concluding the correct conclusion but I ... but that's what it looks like. My group has got the most black population. My group has the most black people. The other classes there's just maybe two, one, two, three but my group has got more than six.* **[HP]**

This informant's perception that her grade was perhaps affected by extraneous factors related to race and ethnicity was endorsed by other informants and was clearly something that had been widely discussed amongst the black and ethnic minority students on the course. One of the white British informants, without identifying the same cause, confirmed the sense of unease triggered by the inexplicitness of the practical assessment criteria:

There were quite a few expressions of shock at people's grades and some niggling about how and why certain people get certain grades compared with other people. Therefore it is unfair from the students' point of view. It wasn't shown to them how they were being marked and assessed what was being marked. A contrast with written assignments where it was clear what the criteria for marking were. **[SJ]**

2. Utilisation of prior knowledge and experience

Another factor affecting how students experienced their teaching and learning contexts, was their sense of how they thought they were perceived by the designers and deliverers of the course. In this respect our informants felt that there were two important issues. Firstly, they felt that very often the content of their course was narrowly ethnocentric in its assumptions of prior deep knowledge of white British Christian traditions and the use of the same sources for illustrative examples. Secondly, our informants felt that they were assumed to have no prior knowledge or experience relevant to their field of study, in this case the hotel and catering and hospitality industry. Apart from the specific family and cultural experiences which students brought to the course, it became quite clear when listening to the informants that they also brought a wide variety of concrete experiences of working in the catering and hospitality industry. All our informants had had such experience and this was not atypical for students generally on the course. However, it seemed that opportunities were being missed for harnessing and integrating this experience within the framework of the course. In a sense the course was constructed with a misleading sense that all the students were necessarily starting from scratch with no previous experience. As one informant put it: '*A lot of lecturers brush off previous experience.*' **[SJ]**

FURTHER CONSIDERATIONS

As we have seen, this study has constantly problematised the category "overseas student", and has identified other, more complex, categories. Nevertheless, after the study had been completed and written up, we decided to have a brief look at the findings of a major research project which had investigated "The Learning Experiences of Overseas Students" (Kinnell 1990). What was remarkable and surprising , was the extent to which this research, focused as it was on "overseas students", and using different research methods, revealed many of the same points of salience and concern. Among these were:- the strong need for constructive feedback and sensitive personal support from lecturers (Kinnell 1990), and the problems of gaining regular access to supervisors (Elsey 1990); the desire to engage in mutual self-help with fellow students (ibid); the difficulty in establishing relationships and friendships with younger British students who were seen as insular and unfriendly (Lewins 1990); the importance of having "the mysteries of academic assessment explained" (Elsey 1990); complaints about the "almost complete absence of anything other than an ethnocentric British view in some areas of study" (ibid); and finally, the severe difficulties, particularly for Ghanaian and Hong Kong Chinese students, in getting tutors to make any kind of effort to pronounce their names correctly or sometimes even to use any name for them at all (Channell 1990).

CONCLUSION

This study, albeit small scale, has yielded supporting evidence for three broad considerations in relation to EAP, questions of ethnicity and aspects of research methodology. Firstly, it has revealed some of the multifaceted complexities involved in the learning contexts for which EAP seeks to provide support. Further, it suggests that areas of concern for EAP should not be restricted to the dimension of skills work. Rather than attention being limited to the façade of EAP, the whole context should be considered and account taken of the subtle and intricate ways in which linguistic factors are inextricably interwoven with societal, cultural and affective ones. Secondly, it is clear that crude categorisations of ethnicity are neither acceptable nor helpful to research into students' learning and perceptions in British higher education. Finally, we believe that this study has shown that there is much to be gained if future, more ambitious studies were to employ ethnographic research methods in this area more extensively, both longitudinally and in terms of depth.

REFERENCES

Archer, C. (1986) Culture bump and beyond. In Valdes, J (ed.) *Culture Bound* C.U.P.

Barge, M. and McCarthy, C. (1995) *"Why is it never right to ask a question?" Cross cultural factors in EAP with particular reference to students from the Far East.* Unpublished paper given at 12th BALEAP conference, Nottingham University March 1995

Bird, J., Sheibani, A. and Francombe, D. (1992) *Ethnic Minorities and Admissions to Higher Education* Bristol Polytechnic

Channell, J. (1990) The Student-Tutor Relationship. In Kinnell, M (ed) *The Learning Experiences of Overseas Students* Open University Press

Elsey, B. (1990) *Teaching and Learning* in *The Learning Experiences of Overseas Students* Open University Press

Evans, C. (1988) *Language People: the Experience of Teaching and Learning Modern Languages in British Universities* Open University Press

Grundy, P. (1993) Student and supervisor perceptions of the role of English in academic success. In Blue, G (ed.) *Language Learning and Success: Studying through English* MEP

Hall, S. (1988) New Ethnicities. In Donald, J & Rattansi, A (eds.) 1992 *'Race', Culture & Difference* Open University/ Sage

Hammersley, M. and Atkinson, P. (1983) *Ethnography: Principles in Practice* Routledge

Haselgrove, S. (1994) *The Student Experience* Open University Press

Kinnell, M. (ed) (1990) *The Learning Experiences of Overseas Students* Open University Press

Lewins, H. (1990) *Living Needs* in *The Learning Experiences of Overseas Students* Open University Press

Thorp, D. (1991) Confused encounters: differing expectations in the EAP classroom. ELT Journal 45:2

English for Very Specific Teaching: Bilateral Gap-filling in British Higher Education or How Can We Internationalise The Staff?

Ann Gavriel
The Robert Gordon University, Aberdeen

INTRODUCTION

The central concern of this paper is how subject lecturers in British universities can internationalise their own standards and expectations, especially in delivery of their syllabus to international students. The title consciously draws upon the analogy of English as a Foreight Language (EFL) 'gap-filling' exercises, where learners are expected to make appropriate language choices in context. The viewpoint expressed here is that these days we should be placing the onus not only on the students to make appropriate choices about language, but also on academic staff themselves. If our aim is to guide students towards successful communication, we must begin by communicating more successfully with them, and 'we' in this context means everyone involved in international education, and not only experts in English for Speakers of Other Lanuages (ESOL).

After visiting a number of gaps between need and provision in terms of 'fit for purpose' language offered by staff to students, the paper moves on to suggest ways of re-assigning some ownership of responsibility for language control among staff at university. Some suggestions as to how this might be done are offered, including staff development events to raise cultural and language awareness, and a recommendation for wider dissemination of ESOL expertise to a more interdisciplinary forum.

THE GAP BETWEEN OLD AND NEW REALITIES

Nowadays British university education for international students has gaps which 'language support' alone cannot fill. Educational needs and student needs are becoming ever more embedded in the tangled undergrowth where language meets culture. Staff should perhaps be less bound up inside the presumptions and assumptions of their own 'academic' subculture; they need to be more flexible and pragmatic in their responses to international student needs. Studying in Britain is for most international students a means to a qualification. Their needs are correspondingly pragmatic and their motivation instrumental. Pragmatics as a branch of sociolinguistics is very much a player here too, since we are concerned with everyone's choice of appropriate language 'code.'

A more pragmatic approach to communication in the learning and teaching environment is appropriate now that we face, in post-binary British higher education, a whole range of new realities. These include:

- underfunding
- wider access and all its ramifications - including recruitment of more international students
- instrumental / vocational motivation (students and staff)
- subject experts who may not be trained or experienced educators

The most immediate effect of these emerging realities is a strongly felt but not often voiced need for staff training and development, especially to enhance communication skills at international level among academic staff. Everyone would agree that university teachers have a responsibility to communicate clearly and competently in a language accessible to the widest possible audience. This responsibility is even more evident now, given the reality of 'wider access' and an international student population across the UK currently averaging between 8 and 10%. The national 'average' is misleading - in some years of some courses at this institution (The Robert Gordon University) the figure is 30% to 50% international students.

The recent changes in higher education have thrown up a number of recurring questions in relation to language support, some of which are presented below. Most of the questions are in some way linked to the premise that awareness of appropriate language choice or use is not solely a matter for the language expert:

- Whose 'perceived' responsibility are language or communication gaps in university education and whose perceptions are we, as ESOL experts, guided by?
- Do students need specific training elements in their course, to equip them for professional practice?
- Are university teachers sufficiently international in their communicating? (And if not, how not, why not?)
- Is EAP still appropriate? Should we not re-tune to English for Specific Purposes (ESP), if only to re-focus on these very specific needs,? And even perhaps to EVP or EPP - English for vocational or professional purposes - whichever suits each different context?

For the purpose of this paper, although all four issues are relevant, discussion is confined to the first three, with the last group of questions providing a backdrop throughout - as a trigger to re-visit in future debate and perhaps to re-think the scope of traditional EAP-based language support provision, in our own context, in the light of matters raised.

There is perhaps a growing awareness in many language support units or departments at universities throughout the UK that an expanding gap exists between need and provision and that this is especially wide in the vocational (or less traditionally 'academic') courses -

technical or industry-linked courses which in the past might have catered mainly for home students. Some of these courses involve placements of six months or a year, out there in the world, where mistakes can cost everyone a lot more than a couple of marks in final assessment.

LEARNING, TRAINING AND LANGUAGE SUPPORT

The English language tutor's work at this university is roughly 75% content-based tuition to international students, much of it on a one-to-one or small group basis. In this context language support is called upon for students in placement as trainee dieticians, architects, pharmacists, nurses, and engineers. Early on in their placements, trainees (for that is what they then are) meet with typical or predictable communication gaps. At such moments the skills required are not 'academic', but undoubtedly belong within the subject syllabus and can be introduced into it through training with some sensitivity and experience about typical language exchange contexts in that field.

Recalling a recent case here, for instance, a Chinese student had arrived in Scotland from Hong Kong six months prior to referral to the English language tutor by her placement supervisor. She had entered directly into the second year of a Nutrition and Dietetics course and at the time of referral for language support found herself on placement training in the local (Aberdeen) hospital. Like most international students who gain advanced admission to the course, she had missed out on the usual induction session offered to first years, which would at least have provided her with a few hours of 'communication skills' to work on a little of the 'culture shock'. In placement allocations such as local hospitals, the cultural and regional 'backdrop' are suddenly in the foreground. One mistake recording information - both from patients or from laboratory staff (particularly over the phone) could cause real harm. In this case, the trainee's work involved taking dietary histories from patients who report meals or use diet-based vocabulary unheard of by the student (e.g. 'neeps & tatties for tea'). The worst case though, and the student's greatest crisis of confidence, occurred when her task was to retrieve and record information at speed, often over the phone. The placement supervisor referred the student for language support after two days in the work place.

Pre-placement training could provide the student with an awareness at least of the amount of 'local research' that needs doing, some familiarity with local names and addresses, regional dietary habits, and strategies for accurate receipt and transmission of information by phone. Because the syllabus did not then make any such provision, English language support was called upon to fill this gap, not pro-actively, but 'remedially', after referral by the placement supervisor, some time into the training.

In fact, a strong case could be made for university course directors to take on the challenge of incorporating far more skills training into the syllabus, to guide students in applying what they gain on the 'academic' side of the course in lectures and seminars. If syllabus remits continue to exclude 'training' - almost as a matter of principle (through a habit of thought connected with the traditional and, I would argue, mistaken, 'education versus training' dichotomy), then the gaps between need and provision for professional practice will prevail.

INTERNATIONALISING THE WRITTEN WORD

Further evidence of a gap between need and provision exists in the case of written instruction from lecturer to student. Here again, students most vulnerable are those who have gained direct entry into an advanced year of the course and have missed out on earlier acculturation.

In addition to the student's lack of cultural background in such cases, there is evidence also that the teaching staff have not considered adapting the written delivery of their courses for the international student population.

Technical subjects such as construction or building surveying have a vast vocabulary which a British student might not see as 'subject terminology'. After all, we have all grown up knowing about skirting boards, chimneys and chimney breasts. For a Malaysian student who has studied quantity surveying in his or her own context, the British building trade vocabulary alone can seem at first impenetrable and afterwards irrelevant to their home context. This is a reasonable enough case for traditional language support, but the gap becomes a bottomless abyss when after only a couple of months here, the student is faced with a deluge of cultural hieroglyphics. It is worth illustrating this point at some length - without wishing to vilify the author of the extracts which follow (whose permission was given to show the extracts for this purpose). Certainly his motives, intentions, and even 'language code' are not judged here as anything less than pure, from a non-international perspective.

The extracts are from a 96-page document - a set of lecture notes and assignment briefs - titled 'Research Method'. The subject is Quantity Surveying. Most of the text is dense with direct and indirect cultural reference (much of it local), innuendo, in-jokes, buzz words, and slightly off-colour humour, swearing and slang. Only a native speaker could appreciate the register, the 'tone', and the way it flits between serious and flippant 'instruction'. Throughout the document any pre-existing concept of 'research' is lampooned in ironic tones which identify in a spirit of camaraderie with the (presumed) attitude of any students reading it. The author is addressing a certain subculture - young British, probably Scottish, male, building trade, a readership suspicious of and unenthusiastic about 'research'. And yet beneath the jibes and jests, the handout - as its length alone will indicate - takes itself very seriously.

As we scan the extracts we can imagine non-native readers searching for 'hard data', useful, clear and concise guidelines. And as teaching professionals, we are driven to ask : What does it teach? How does it instruct? What are its aims? Does it achieve any of them?

Extracts (from BSc Surveying Course Document 'Research Method')

Extract 1 [from Section headed '*What Research is*']

> *... For example, you want to know when architects and brickys begin to hate each other so deeply and profoundly. You hypothesise that they learn this skill in their first year at college ...*
>
> *... So that's roughly what research is, and isn't. And you thought it was going to be boring! Please let me do some research I hear you cry as, drooling slightly in anticipation of the sheer orgasmic pleasure, you desperately crave a research methods assignment. Have patience, yet do not despair...*

Extract 2 [from a Section called '*Brief in Relation to Honours Work*']

> *... Unless you fancy hanging around here into your dotage, or have access to a team of highly qualified slaves, your IBP would need to be considerably more limited than this ...*

> *... Anyone having difficulty in thinking of anything they are interested in will be allocated the In-depth hands-on olfactory analysis of the Aberdeen sewer system ...*

Extract 3 [from a Section *'Defining Real-World Problems for Research'*]

> *"The purpose of this study will be to analyse the motets of Palestrina ..."*
>
> *Can anyone out there explain to me what this quote means? The old buffer is trying to give us all a clear idea of how to define a research project ... I would also suggest it doesn't represent the kind of real world problem that you are likely to be pursuing in your research. However, each to their own, and perhaps a skilled gynaecologist might want to analyse poor old Palestrina's motets.*

Many of the students given this text were Chinese Malaysians, but I should add that even European Exchange (ERASMUS) students with Proficiency level English were at a loss to interpret such a heavy wodge of cultural narcissism.

Students reading sciences or engineering within the traditional 'arts-sciences' binary system did not enter their fields because they enjoyed writing about it, nor probably did they see themselves as 'good verbalisers' - good at the language arts. This fundamental division not only lives on, but seems to be universal, and so it is entirely understandable that international students on technical, scientific, 'vocational' or design-based courses, do not greedily nor speedily come to terms with screeds of densely-packed text, either as reader or author. They expect that handouts will be helpful and instructive. They take seriously everything that is given them to read at university. Even if warned (by the lecturer) that a lot of it is 'jokey', humour does not move comfortably across cultures even if we work at it. So for non-British students, the jokey bits are just more incomprehensible bits. A student's serious reading load is hefty enough, without having to plough through a almost a hundred pages of 'humour' targeted at another readership entirely (the British quantity surveying apprentices) for the sake of a dozen pages at most of research method guidelines. Between and along every line of his handout, the author had coded the message*: 'I know where you're at, lads, 'cos I've been there too ...* 'but this affirmation of fellowship was lost entirely on the non-British students. It cannot be emphasised enough though that the author did not intend any exclusion of international students. He simply had not realised, had not imagined, that it would be so inappropriate for them.

A more general question arising from this quantity surveying illustration concerns the responsibility each educator has as role model among students. If the language of lecturers functions, albeit unwittingly, as a segregator of home and non-home students, then home students could also feel less prepared and less obliged to adapt their own language codes to include their non-local peers.

COMMUNICATION AWARENESS AND ASSESSMENT OF WRITTEN WORK

If subject staff become conscious of the content and cultural register of their own writing, it will undoubtedly be beneficial to them as well as their students. It might encourage in them a more general 'language awareness' and since written work is still the main form of assessment, and they the assessors, this could be significant. Very few subject lecturers give guiding comments on students' written work other than the more 'intuitive', often negative note such as 'poor English', 'you need to improve your English', or 'I cannot understand your English'. In some cases the student may have just one recurring error (subject-verb agreement springs to mind) but if the lecturer marking the assignment does not know that, as far as s/he is concerned the script is a mass of different grammatical problems.

Precisely because these otherwise astute 'expert users' of English might concede that explicit language correction is not within their expertise, evaluative comments on the student's use of the language are always unhelpful and inappropriate. Much more helpful would be a focused comment identifying the type of language expected, with a note suggesting that more specific grammatical points could be worked on with the language tutor. It is then, sure enough, up to the 'language repair person' to fix this student's 'poor English' - but we should not have to keep patching up the shattered confidence as well. There has to be some movement towards a more discourse-enlightened staff in this university culture which still assesses a student's achievement, on the basis of how competently they write. It is not the language experts who hold sway at that stage.

To further compound these very complex issues, we British are perhaps more attuned to 'placing' each other through speech and language use than many other cultures. But internationally, most people perceive and protect their own identify through a strong attachment to the way they speak and their cultural background - so that any allusion to their language skills, no matter how sensitively offered, can be construed as an assault on them personally, on their speech, idiolect, regional accent, or regional identity. Before making 'appropriate language' overtures to anyone at all therefore, we should be very conscious of how the different regions, countries and socio-culturally distinct groups within the UK perceive their own 'language identity'. This question of 'the right approach' is in many ways the crux of the matter.

THE CHANGING ROLE OF ESOL EXPERTS

The first question arising from all of these concerns is:
How are academic staff across the UK facing up to these responsibilities?

A second but related question is:
How are we, from an Applied Linguistics or ESOL perspective, helping them to take on this new challenge?

The role of the ESOL expert within a growing international student population is changing. The contention of this paper is that one of our main aims these days is to internationalise codes of communication in all university courses. We must begin to propagate our knowledge and experience at the language-culture interface.

RECOMMENDATIONS

The following are some suggestions and recommendations on how can we be most effective in propagating knowledge about the language-culture interface.

Sharing the expertise in our own work place

Are ESOL experts invited to share knowledge and perceptions with academic staff? Perhaps they are, but as information or advice givers on English language entrance requirements, English examination IELTS scores, and so on, or as report writers on referred students. Are they invited to give guidance on how best to teach international students, on how to implement 'best practice' to benefit all members of the student population (and this question applies even if language proficiency is at an acceptable level on entry)? If not, why not? In many universities the English language support service accepts unquestioningly the mantle of Cinderella to faculties and departments. Even if the service is provided by an Applied Linguistics Department with active and eminent researchers in the field of language teaching, there is still a rather apologetic reluctance to pass on the baton of language awareness as part of staff training and development. But it makes much more sense to start doing just that.

It is time to share the expertise, to disseminate more widely and thus to share the increasing burden on traditional language support staff. Cultural awareness is a good place to start, since from within that framework many delicate matters can be broached, such as how lecturers perceive their educational responsibilities to international students.

At The Robert Gordon University, a sharing of expertise is already underway. A staff training and development programme, the Initiative on Cultural Awareness in the Learning Environment, is in its third year of highly valued forums, seminars and workshops. Its aims and objectives are to:

- introduce the idea of specialist training (preparation) of international students for particular communicative events - e.g. formal presentations, placement situations, practical assessment

- raise awareness about the language-culture 'interface' - including what counts as 'culture' and how using a type of English which is culturally coded has the effect of unwittingly excluding non-members of that language community

- help to 'internationalise' heavily culture-soaked parts of their courses, lecture notes, assignment briefs, and even exam questions, by introducing language awareness seminars and workshops

- teach what is teachable in terms of text organisation, discourse conventions, expectations, criteria and guidelines in the assessment of student writing - so that criticism of assignments can be constructive and instructive, rather than negative ("You need to improve your English", "Poor English").

Reaching out into the world of higher education

Specialist conferences attract specialists. At BALEAP gatherings we are here for a couple of days to communicate with each other, to 'preach to the converted' and to mingle with other specialists. But what we disseminate among ourselves is of even more value to university lecturers, trainers and non-ESOL experts. The vast history we have of teaching to and learning from international audiences has equipped the ESOL profession uniquely to pass on a more interculturally accessible style of education. We are not simply about syntax and spelling.

Would it be too impracticable to call for a truly interdisciplinary conference just once a year? If we agree that it is time to preach to the 'unconverted', then perhaps that would be the first step.

So, both in-house and externally, we can address these questions. We can set up workshops and seminars, making use of video, interviews, and surveys. We can inform other academics about the differing cultural profiles of students while at the same time exposing and resisting the tendency to create stereotypes.

This is part of what is meant in this paper by 'internationalising' our standards and expectations. Standards have gained currency recently in the buzz-word sense of 'maintaining quality' - and though that is not really what is meant in this context, the quality of education itself is undeniably affected by the language used to deliver it. If we are welcoming international students on courses which are relevant to their needs, then we cannot at the same time expect them to suffer the consequences of neglecting to make the syllabus internationally accessible. An assumption of 'universal' practice and behaviour is implicit in many subjects, even though what is taught is culturally British. Perhaps it is still imperialistically assumed that what is British is, or damn-well ought to be, universal.

Cultural awareness - a final word

To illustrate the effect of a particular type of cultural assumption - that what we (British) mean by a concept must be what 'they' (the rest of the world) mean by it too - I offer an example which concerned a talented Malaysian student who had been admitted directly into the third year of the Architecture BSc Honours course. The student had become sullen and was behaving 'out of character'. He said he was unable to get his ideas across to a tutor who had set him his first assignment. He felt that the tutor was not even listening to his design arguments. The lecturer's seemingly very straightforward brief had directed students to design a housing complex "for first-time buyers". All the connotations embedded in that cultural reference were assumed to be universal. If you knew the meanings of the words, you understood the concept. However, to a young Malaysian from a professional, middle-class family, 'first-time buyers' also typically means young newly-weds, but instead of a house on a budget, their first home is a dream love nest - no expense spared. So what (in architectural terms) amounted to 'over-designing' for the British brief, was in fact quite a modest response by Malaysian standards.

The most valuable lesson to be learnt from encounters at the language-culture interface is a willingness to examine our assumptions before acting - before delivering syllabuses, for example. As part of their job, ESOL professionals are good at guessing what is being assumed by whom and why. The time is ripe to share the experience, to teach subject staff how to look carefully through their own language and its cultural messages and to reflect on the need for more care in communicating, so as not to exclude international members of the group. Not just the message but also its context must be made explicit Home students receiving the same explicit language might also gain an insight - about the need sometimes to 'state the obvious' for the sake of those we are welcoming into our group.

REFERENCES

Ballard, B. (1983) 'Improving student writing: an integrated approach to cultural adjustment' ELT Docs 117 British Council/CUP

Briggs, S. (1987) 'When course success varies from discourse success' *ESP* 1987 6/2

Criper, C and Davies, A. (1988) *English Language Testing Service (ELTS) Validation Report,* Research Report 1(I) (University of Edinburgh), Sections 6 and 7 (Supervisors' judgements) pbr: British Council and University of Cambridge LES

Farrington, O. (1981) 'The first five seconds: the ESP teacher and 'out-of-the-blue' language *ELT Docs 112*, British Council/CUP

Gavriel, A. (1990) 'An exploration of contrastive rhetoric as a tool for cultural awareness raising in British higher education' unpublished MA thesis, ELT Department, Ealing College (now Thames Valley University), London

Gavriel, A. (1994) Academic Staff Survey concerning international students at Robert Gordon University, Aberdeen (unpublished)

Lynch, T. (1994) 'Training lecturers for international audiences' in

Flowerdew, J. (ed.) *Academic Listening: Research Perspectives*, CUP

Prodromou, L. (1988) 'English as cultural action' ELTJ April 88

Swales, J. (1982) 'Examining examination papers', *English Language Research Journal* 1982/3

Valdes, J. Merrill (1987) *Culture Bound,* Cambridge University Press

Degree EAP: More Than a Status Change

Paul Fanning
Middlesex University

INTRODUCTION

In British Universities, courses in English for Academic Purposes (EAP) are usually separated from students' "main" studies to a greater or lesser extent. A course will be totally separate if it is optional (albeit strongly recommended for the most needy students), powerless to affect overall assessment grades, added to (rather than replacing) other courses, and, as in Skeldon and Swales' (1983) experience, given the lowest timetabling priority.

The separateness of the EAP course can be reduced through a variety of devices, such as making successful grades a condition for progression with the other studies (as happens, for example, on many pre-sessional EAP courses in British universities), or arranging for in-sessional EAP grades to affect overall semester/year grades in some way. However, true integration of EAP courses is not achieved until they become a full substitute for an established degree course component or module, rather than just a "tacked on" addition. Such integration means that the EAP will not entail special, additional study for the students who take it, and that the EAP grade will affect progression and averages as much as any other grade. Integration to this extent is extremely rare in Britain.

Sometimes it can be difficult to recognise that an EAP course is not fully integrated within a degree programme. In my own institution there used to be a course offered as part of a First Year BA in European Business Administration. Many of the criteria for proper integration within the overall degree were met: the final grade was in the same form and had the same weighting as grades for other components; students had to obtain a pass in order to progress to Year Two; the course grade appeared on students' transcripts.

However, there was a problem with the amount of time that the students were expected to devote to the English component. They were aware that they studied more modules than students on other courses, and they believed that it was the English module that made the difference. Therefore, they would carry out coursework assignments, but little other private study, on the grounds that their "main" Business Studies programme was too heavy. After all, they had applied to study for a Business degree, and saw English as "tacked onto" that.

It is not difficult to see why British EAP has not traditionally been integrated into degree programmes. Its original justification only arose after overseas students began to arrive in Britain to study in existing degree programmes. It was not a reason for students to go to Britain, but a reaction to problems that they encountered on arrival. Its relation to other subjects is a dependent one, as its name indicates. Nor has it traditionally been seen as particularly "academic" (in terms of intellectual demands made), especially at the postgraduate level typical for the majority of its early students.

Today, the possibility of incorporating EAP into a wider degree programme is growing. Various reasons can be found for this. Most obviously there is the growing trend towards modularisation in British universities, which makes EAP-sized courses easier to fit in. Secondly, EAP is becoming more common amongst undergraduate students, who are more likely to be able to accommodate a less academic "skills"-type course in the early part of their courses. And thirdly, as Blue & Archibald (this volume) show, there are many more EU students in British universities, students who are more concerned than traditional overseas students to study English while in Britain.

My claim in this paper is that EAP fully incorporated into a formal degree programme is a very different ball-game from the more free-standing kind that is normally described. It brings undoubted benefits, but makes special demands too. I shall first describe some general effects on EAP of degree status, and then examine in detail one these effects - guaranteed private study time - because of its important pedagogical implications.

GENERAL EFFECTS OF FULL EAP INTEGRATION

These may be listed as follows:

1. Guaranteed time for private study (directed/self-directed)
2. Greater learner motivation.
3. Relevance of institutional quality-control procedures.
4. Need to appear "academic"
5. Difficulty of syllabus negotiation
6. Less need for free-standing classes

1. Guaranteed time for private study

The amount of time that learners can devote to private study is directly related to the extent of integration of the EAP course within a degree programme. Where there is no integration at all, the learners' "main" subjects will usually form a complete full-time degree course by themselves, leaving no time in theory for any other kind of study. That learners even find time to come to an EAP class, let alone put in extra hours doing homework, is a bonus for them and their EAP tutors.

At the other extreme, full integration of EAP demands that students spend as much time on their EAP as on any other course component. In my own institution we base our calculations on the assumption that a full-time student should spend about 36 hours per week on classes and private study. Students are expected to take 3 modules per semester. Thus, when EAP is one of the three, it merits one-third of 36 hours per week, i.e. 12 hours. Since modules normally involve 3 class contact hours per week, the private study requirement is 9 hours.

2. Greater learner motivation

Learners' motivation is likely to be greater in several respects when EAP has degree status. Firstly, the learners will probably have a greater interest in the target language and culture *per se* - greater integrative motivation in the terms of Gardner and Lambert (1972). Any such increase will result not so much from the course as from a change in the composition of the class which in our experience contains a different mix of students. Our degree class needs to be accompanied by an extracurricular class containing students who clearly do not wish to make the extra commitment to English entailed by signing up for a formal module and, therefore, lack the integrative motivation of the degree class.

Secondly, degree EAP is likely, by the way it is organized, to increase learners' instrumental motivation. According to Skehan (1989), instrumental motivation may be characterised as increases beyond a pre-existing internal level of motivation that result from external influences and incentives. The most obvious external influence brought to bear by degree EAP is the assessment hurdles that it imposes. A more subtle one, perhaps, might be the promise of greater general success as a student flowing from participation in a more serious and intensive EAP course.

3. Relevance of institutional quality control procedures

Institutional quality-control procedures have been greatly increased, but a non-degree EAP course could be excluded. (If there are quality-control procedures for non-degree EAP, they are likely to result from the initiative of the EAP department, one of whose options is the impressive BALEAP scheme for accrediting pre-sessional EAP courses). Degree EAP, however, has little choice about how its quality is monitored. Like most other degree course components it has to deal with external examiners, end-of-course student feedback, annual monitoring reports, course boards of study, funding body audits and the like. Quality-control may apply to any EAP course, but its rigour is guaranteed if the EAP is fully integrated into a degree.

4. Need to appear "academic"

The need to appear academic stems from the tendency of EAP in general to lack respectability because it is seen, justifiably or not, as "remedial", "training", "servicing", or "skills-based" - labels considered pejorative in many higher education circles. Non-degree EAP may be able to survive such attitudes, but once academic credits are involved EAP must show that it has something else. This something else may always in fact have been present, or may be new.

Courses can be shown to be academic in different ways. One way is to demonstrate that subject matter and task types are typical of what is encountered in the academic environment. An "academic" course would thus deal with "issues", such as "development vs environment", rather than everyday descriptions like "what I did for my holiday"; and tasks like essay-writing and summaries, rather than composing postcard messages.

Since subject-relevant content and task types are major criteria for "face validity" in ESP courses (a transparent link with the learners' target language situation), and since many EAP courses anyway recognise a need for face validity in order to motivate their students, it is clear that the need to seem "academic" in this sense already exists to some extent in EAP courses. However, this need will be strengthened when EAP is integrated within a degree.

Another way to make degree EAP seem more "academic" is to include some more theoretical study of language and/or study skills ("language awareness" in the words of Turner, 1993). The problem here, however, is that time for skills practice is short, and increased focus on theoretical knowledge may cost too much of this valuable practice. Finally, mention should be made of Widdowson's contention (1983) that if ESP courses become closer to "education" than "training" the less specific they are. Widdowson advises that EAP courses in particular have a need to be educational (surely a similar idea to "academic"), and can achieve this by not being too specific.

5. Difficulty of syllabus negotiation

Syllabus negotiation is defined by Bloor and Bloor (1988) as "helping students arrive at the position of being able to understand and articulate their language learning objectives". Of its nature, it involves delaying finalisation of course details until after the students have arrived to take the course. It is this characteristic of syllabus negotiation which makes its adoption more difficult by degree EAP. Bloor and Bloor (ibid) argue that even ESP courses which do not "have to run the gauntlet of degree committees and senate vetting" are nevertheless under pressure to finalise course details well in advance of the learners' arrival. Courses which do have to satisfy university quality control committees are that much more pressured to avoid syllabus negotiation.

6. Less need for free-standing classes

By free-standing classes I mean sessions which start and complete a learning topic on the same occasion. This type of class is often essential in more optional EAP courses because of the irregularity of learners' attendance. (If a course topic is allowed to carry over to a subsequent class, there is every chance that many of the learners will miss its completion or start it half-way through, thus increasing the risk that they will have wasted their time). Converting the EAP into a degree course in its own right, however, reduces the need for free-standing classes, as regular learner attendance is much more guaranteed.

Having now detailed some general effects on EAP of its integration as a full undergraduate degree component, I move on to consider how one of these effects - guaranteed private study time for the students - itself impacts on EAP pedagogy in a number of important ways.

EFFECTS OF GUARANTEED PRIVATE STUDY TIME

There are four particular such effects that I wish to consider:

1. Different use of class time.
2. Increased need for self-access learning.
3. Stronger case for learner training
4. Extra preparation and marking for the tutor.

1. Different use of class time

When an in-sessional EAP course is not part of a degree, learners typically undertake very little private study. Therefore, all of the work must be carried out in class. The learners will not usually question the nature of the classwork unless it seems irrelevant to their needs. If, however, private study is possible and expected, then there may be more pressure on the tutor to consider the best use of her/his time with students, and to identify work which could be just as well carried out by the learners on their own. I personally was censured once by a student over using class time for individual writing leading up to a class discussion. The student saw the discussion as the primary learning activity, and asked why I had not set the writing as preparatory homework in order to leave more time for discussion.

It is clear from such experiences that some classroom activities are more "legitimate" than others. Two obvious criteria for legitimacy are dependence on other learners and dependence on the tutor. Based on these criteria, we might list (besides discussions) the following as "legitimate" class activities: introducing private study tasks (presenting the requisite knowledge, explaining the nature of the task), evaluating answers to private study tasks, class tests, oral presentations, group writing, and (possibly) learner training.

Tutor-supervised self-access (where learners themselves choose materials, topics and/or tasks) is considered to be logically a non-legitimate use of class contact time. This is primarily because self-access work can be fairly easily carried out without the presence of either a tutor or other learners. St John (1988) lists possible tutor roles in tutored self-access as "to organize the material and access to it; to provide answer sheets; to provide guidance, explanations, help at the students' request". In addition to this, a tutor's presence might sometimes be seen as a way to guarantee the actual accomplishment of self-access work. However, these advantages do not make the tutor indispensable. Many self-access centres nowadays are staffed by non-academic receptionists who can provide all necessary guidance on finding and using material. And student attendance can be encouraged by devices such as student record books, as described by St John (1988) or Cotterall (1995).

2. Increased need for self-access learning

Self-access study is important in degree EAP for more reasons than just the intrinsic benefits described by Cotterall (1995). Self-access work is in tune with the general philosophy of undergraduate degrees (that students should take responsibility for their own learning), and it relieves course tutors of the impractical task of providing enough materials for 8-9 hours per week of set homework.

It will probably be necessary to promote and monitor self-access study, because its enhanced importance is not a sufficient condition to ensure that it will actually get done. Student record books are a useful device for monitoring as well as the promotion mentioned above. For further promotion, the tutor can make individualised study suggestions in feedback on course tasks. This works best in conjunction with a well-equipped self-access centre; with ours only partially complete we have drawn up a wide-ranging bibliography of potentially useful library materials categorised under broad problem headings such as "Study Skills", "Grammar" or "Listening". Another promotional technique is to use class time to introduce a range of different study activities, telling learners to complete in their own time whichever they find the most interesting or potentially helpful. We also repeatedly highlight interesting ways in which the learners can take advantage of living in an English-speaking country, for example by joining a public library, going regularly to the cinema, or making British friends.

3. Stronger case for learner training

Dickinson's (1988) definition of learner training hints at its unsuitability for non-degree in-sessional EAP. Two of Dickinson's key requirements for suitability - expectations of autonomous learning and amount of study time - are likely to be minimal if EAP courses are outside a degree programme. Degree EAP, on the other hand, will have a much greater need for learner training because both factors are very significant. The role of learner training is not just to facilitate directed language learning, but also to encourage self-directed learning.

4. Extra preparation and marking for the tutor

It is self-evident that if the learners engage in more private study the tutor will have to prepare and mark more. This is in itself no bad thing in terms of course quality (students maximising their use of expert help), but of course it has to be accompanied by a corresponding reduction in the tutor's duties elsewhere to make room for the extra time necessitated. If EAP's elevation to degree status creates an intolerable burden for the tutor, then the quality of the tutor's input will suffer. The effect on tutor workload of a change in course status should therefore be carefully considered.

CONCLUSION

It is clear that with so many pedagogical effects, the change in the status of EAP from "support" to full degree component is a drastic but perhaps worthwhile one. However, it is not always easy to achieve a genuine change. Too often in EAP we are fobbed off with a quasi-incorporation within the academic programme, where in fact the EAP is "tacked on" to a self-contained degree instead of replacing an existing component. The time for learners' private study, with all its dependent effects, will be a particular casualty in such cases.

One question that I have frequently considered in seeking out a pedagogy for degree EAP is whether I am merely reinventing the wheel that has been familiar for decades to those who run degree (and indeed school) programmes in foreign languages other than English (e.g. Mason, 1970; Beattie, 1987). Degree EAP could, after all, be viewed as just another university-level foreign language course. What I hope makes my conclusions worth considering is the perspective that I have presented: the contrast with non-degree university EAP. This contrast might also be of interest to teachers of other foreign languages given the trend in today's British universities to introduce so-called "open language" classes - optional extracurricular foreign language classes for entire student populations.

REFERENCES

Beattie, N. (1987). Homework in the teaching and learning of Modern Languages. *British Journal of Language Teaching*: 67-72.

Bloor, M. and Bloor, T. (1988). Syllabus negotiation: the basis of learner autonomy. In A. Brookes and P. Grundy (eds) *Individualization and Autonomy in Language Learning*. MEP/British Council.

Cotterall, S. (1995). A course strategy for learner autonomy. *English Language Teaching Journal*, 49,3: 219-227.

Dickinson, L. (1988). Learner training. In A. Brookes and P. Grundy (eds) *Individualization and Autonomy in Language Learning*. MEP/British Council.

Gardner, R. and Lambert, W. (1972). *Attitudes and Motivation in Second Language Learning*. Rowley, Mass: Newbury House.

Mason, H.T. (1970). The requirements of the university. In C.V. Russell (ed) *Post-O'Level Studies in Modern Languages*. Oxford : Pergamon.

Skehan, P. (1989). *Individual Differences in Foreign Language Learning*. London : E. Arnold.

Skeldon, P. and Swales, J. (1981). Working with service English timetables. *English Language Teaching Journal*, 37, 2 : 138-144

St John, M. (1988). Attitudinal changes to self-access in ESP. In A. Brookes and P. Grundy (eds) *Individualization and Autonomy in Language Learning*. MEP/British Council.
Turner, J. (1993). EAP: peripheral current or mainstream flow? In G. Blue (ed) *Language Learning and Success: Studying through Writing*. London, MacMillan.
Widdowson, H. (1983). *Learning Purpose and Language Use*. Oxford: OUP

The Europeanisation of the EAP Classroom

George Blue and Alasdair Archibald
University of Southampton

INTRODUCTION

In recent years there have been considerable changes in the composition of the international student body in British universities. This paper seeks to document some of these changes, drawing particular attention to the recent growth in numbers of European students. It reports on a questionnaire study carried out among visiting students and discusses the implications of the findings for the teaching of English for Academic Purposes (EAP).

INTERNATIONAL STUDENTS IN BRITISH UNIVERSITIES

Before the foundation of BALEAP (or SELMOUS as it was then known) the number of students from abroad in British universities were relatively small, and the majority were from Commonwealth countries.

In 1972, the year SELMOUS was founded, the number of students coming from 'foreign' countries overtook the number from Commonwealth countries for the first time (Albert 1976, cited in Weir 1983). This had profound implications as far as the need for English language provision was concerned, as for most of these students English was a *foreign* language, whereas for the Commonwealth students it was mostly a *second* language. Consequently, during the next ten years many of the 'old' universities appointed full-time specialists in English for overseas students to help these students cope with the demands of studying through the medium of a foreign language. The five founder SELMOUS universities of 1972 had grown to twelve member universities by 1982. During this same period many universities introduced or strengthened their English language admissions requirements for students whose mother tongue and language of education were not English, and by 1982 the British Council/UCLES ELTS Test was available in British Council offices worldwide (having replaced the Davies Test in 1980).

In fact, proportionally, Commonwealth student numbers held their own during the 1970s. This decade saw substantial growth in international student numbers generally, at least until 1979, the year that 'full cost' overseas student fees were announced, when the total number of students from abroad reached 82,400 (a figure not to be exceeded until 1990 and still not exceeded as far as non-European Union (EU) students are concerned). By 1982 the number of students from abroad had dropped to 56,600 (Figure 1), but we see the beginnings of the growth in the numbers of European students, from less than 4% (or only 3,000) European Community (EC) students in 1979 to 11% (6,200) in 1982.

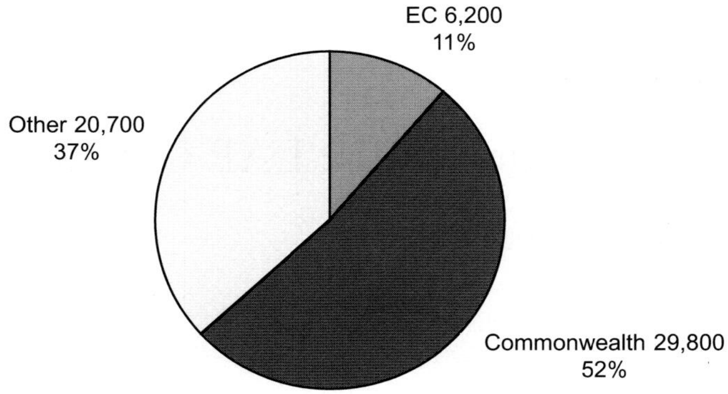

Figure 1. Total students from abroad in Great Britain 1982

If we jump another ten years to 1992 we find considerable growth both in the numbers of students from abroad and in the English language provision that universities make available, with some 52 institutions (or half of all universities) now belonging to BALEAP.

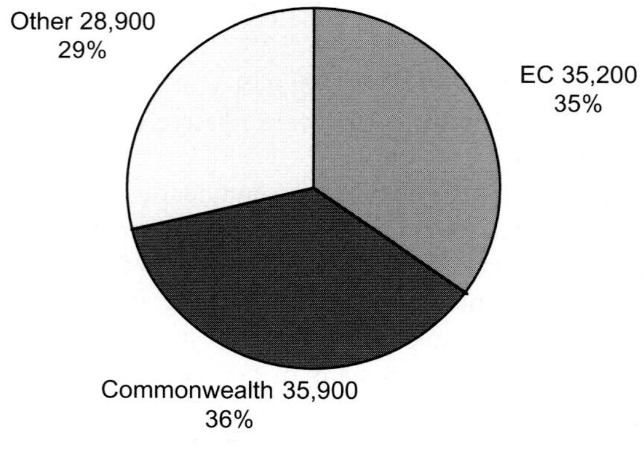

Figure 2. Total students from abroad in Great Britain 1992

During the decade 1982-92 there was a 20% increase in the numbers of Commonwealth students, a 40% increase in the numbers of 'other' students and a spectacular 468% increase in the numbers of EC students (Figure 2). Table 1 shows the 'top ten' countries for 1992, with their student numbers and positions for 1982 alongside.

By 1992 there were five EC countries, three Commonwealth countries and two 'others' in the top 10 sending countries, and three of the top five countries were members of the (now) European Union. In 1982 only two EC countries had been in the top 10, compared with five Commonwealth countries and three 'others'. During the decade France, Ireland and Spain (all EC countries by 1992 though Spain was not a member in 1982) saw their numbers rise dramatically, whereas Brunei, Iran and Iraq dropped out of the top 10 (the latter two perhaps not surprisingly), and Nigeria dropped from third place (with 4,600 students in Britain) to 23rd place (with only 900). Japan was the only non-EU country to enter the top ten during this period.

Table 1. Top Ten Countries 1992

		1992	*1982*	*1982 position*
1	Malaysia	8,500	7,500	(1st)
2	Hong Kong	7,300	6,600	(2nd)
3	Germany	7,300	1,200	(8th)
4	France	6,700	800	(15th)
5	Greece	6,200	2,400	(6th)
6	USA	5,200	2,700	(5th)
7	Ireland	4,700	500	(23rd)
8	Singapore	3,400	1,100	(9th)
9	Spain	3,300	200	(position unknown)
10	Japan	2,500	400	(position unknown)

Source: Department for Education (1994)

INTERNATIONAL STUDENTS AT THE UNIVERSITY OF SOUTHAMPTON

In common with other British universities Southampton experienced a growth in numbers of students from abroad in the period in question, and in recent years Language Centre staff have been aware of a sharp increase in the numbers of EU students attending English language classes. Many of these EU students are in fact visiting students, mostly on an ERASMUS/ SOCRATES exchange.

As far as pre-sessional[1] courses are concerned, the figures show a steady increase from 20% EC students in 1984, to 29% in 1989, to 45% EU students in 1994. If we take six selected countries, we can see from Table 2 how the balance of students attending the pre-sessional course has changed:

Table 2. Students from 6 Countries on Pre-Sessional Courses

Country	*1984*	*1989*	*1994*
Brazil	4	2	1
Egypt	6	5	2
France	1	1	8
Germany	1	5	9
Greece	9	6	21
Italy	0	5	8

[1] A pre-sessional course is a preparatory course usually focusing on English language and academic study skills taken prior to students' registration on their subject specific academic programme of study.

When we come to look at the numbers enrolling for in-sessional[2] classes we find that in 1994-95 48% of the *registered* students (i.e. those taking Southampton degrees) were from EU countries, whilst 88% of the *visiting* students were from the EU. 61% of students enrolled for EAP classes, which are primarily run for the benefit of registered students, were in fact visiting students. Overall, 73% of *all* students enrolled for in-sessional EAP courses were from EU countries in the first semester of 1994-95, with Germany accounting for 17%, Italy 12%, France 11% and Greece 10%.

It can be seen, then, that in Britain as a whole there are large numbers of EU students in the University system, a situation that is borne out by the Southampton experience. Where they are able to do so these EU students are inevitably making heavy demands on universities' EAP provision and perhaps even changing the nature of that provision - possibly making it more difficult for some of the non-EU students to derive full benefit from it.

THE ORGANISATION OF IN-SESSIONAL CLASSES AT SOUTHAMPTON

In common with many other British Universities Southampton offers free in-sessional English language classes to students for whom English is not the mother tongue and language of education. Students following Southampton degree courses must first satisfy the admissions office that they have an adequate level of linguistic competence, normally by taking an approved test (most commonly IELTS or TOEFL) or by satisfactorily completing a pre-sessional course. Consequently, these classes have traditionally been at a fairly advanced level and have tended to be academically oriented. Classes have tended to have a skills focus and have included *Reading and Study Skills*, *Academic Writing*, *Listening and Note Making*, as well as more general classes in areas such as *Grammar* and *Pronunciation*. In recent years, *Proficiency Level English* has been added mainly for the visiting students, together with *English in the News*, aimed directly at them. In addition to these classes, all students have been able to sign up for an individual twenty-minute tutorial (normally for help with academic writing) on a weekly or less frequent basis.

By October 1994 there was a growing concern that EAP classes originally aimed at students following Southampton degree courses were being filled with visiting students. Not only are the needs and expectations of these students different from those of the registered students, but there can also be considerable differences in the level of language proficiency. It was therefore decided to run two separate programmes: one for registered students and the other for visiting students.

The number of registered students who enrolled for in-sessional classes in the first semester was 62 (rather lower than in previous years). Of these, 30 (48%) were European and 32 (52%) non-European. On the other hand, the number of visiting students enrolling for English language classes was even higher than in previous years. 99 visiting students enrolled in the first semester, of whom 87 (88%) were European and 12 (12%) non-European. As already pointed out, 73% of *all* students enrolled for in-sessional EAP courses were from EU countries. In the remainder of this paper, though, we shall be focusing on the 99 visiting students, who accounted for 61% of all students enrolled for English language classes.

---

[2] In-sessional classes are EAP support classes for students already registered on their academic programme of study.

THE QUESTIONNAIRE STUDY

Many of the decisions that have been made concerning language provision for visiting students have been in response to rapidly changing circumstances, and they have lacked the careful planning and detailed needs analysis that would normally be considered necessary. Even in setting up a separate programme for visiting students we were conscious of the fact that we were offering these students what we thought they needed and wanted, informed to some extent by experience and informal discussions with visiting students, but not determined in a very rigorous manner. The purpose of the questionnaire study was therefore to discover more about the visiting students so that future decisions could be better informed. A secondary aim was to present some of this information to the University in the hope that some central funding could be found for language courses for visiting students (this in fact turned out to be a vain hope).

A questionnaire was designed and was piloted with a group attending the *English in the News* class. In the light of comments made by this group some changes were made. Questionnaires were then sent to the 99 visiting students enrolled for English language classes in the last two weeks of the first semester.

By the start of the second semester 21 responses had been received, and we proceeded to analyse these. We decided to reject two of them as the respondents did not match our definition of visiting student. The results reported below are therefore based on 19 responses, representing about 20% of the visiting students enrolled for in-sessional classes.

Results of the questionnaire study

Eight of the respondents were male and 11 female. Their ages ranged from 20 to 28 years, with a mean age of 23 years. The respondents were all from the EU: eight German, five French, three Italian, two Spanish and one Portuguese. Ten were studying in the Faculty of Social Sciences, five in the Science Faculty, two in Arts, one in Mathematics and one in Engineering. The questions can be broadly grouped under three headings: motivation, integration and language learning.

Motivation

We shall consider two questions under this heading, concerning students' motivation to come to the UK in the first place and their motivation for learning English.

Many respondents gave more than one reason for coming to Britain. However, 15 of the 19 (79%) included learning English as a major reason. One response serves well to sum up what many obviously felt:

> *'basically to learn the language.'*

Another very important motivation cited by 11 respondents (58%) was to do with British culture and way of life. Responses included:

> *'to make some experiences with the culture'*

> *'interest in the culture and heritage of the country'*

'experiencing new styles of life'.

Only six (32%) gave academic reasons, for example:

'poor Chemistry Department in [home university]'

'knowing another way of studying'

'to obtain experience in my field'.

Finally, a further nine gave other reasons which were not easy to categorise, including:

'to spend a year abroad'

'opportunity to make new friends'

'ERASMUS grant'.

It appears that there is an element of coming to study in Britain simply because the opportunity exists!

Another open-ended question asked about their reasons for wanting to improve their English, and many respondents gave more than one reason. The most common type of reason was to do with social integration, cited by nine respondents (47%):

'to be better integrated in the English society'

'I didn't want to be recognised as a foreigner as soon as I opened my mouth'

'to understand and be able to talk to your friends'.

In Gardner and Lambert's (1972) terms these types of response would represent an integrative orientation, reflecting 'an inquisitiveness and genuine interest in the people comprising a cultural group' or possibly even a 'willingness or a desire to be like representative members of the 'other' language group' (1972).

At the other end of the scale two categories of reasons were very much more instrumental, reflecting 'the practical value and advantages of learning a new language' or 'a desire to gain social recognition or economic advantages through knowledge of a foreign language' (Gardner and Lambert 1972). Five respondents (26%) cited professional reasons, e.g.:

'crucial for the job later on'

'career opportunities'

The same number gave academic reasons (26%):

'many physics books are written in English'

'to pass exams'.

Finally, nine respondents (47%) gave a variety of other reasons which were not so easy to categorise. Some of these seemed to be of a fairly instrumental nature, including the role of English as an international language:

> *'English is the most spoken language'*

> *'All the world speaks English, especially the scientific world'.*

Others clearly reflected a more integrative orientation, e.g.:

> *'English is no more considered to be a foreign language: it's a sort of self understanding to speak English fluently'.*

Still others could have been interpreted in either way, e.g.:

> *'I want to know as many languages as possible as good as possible'*

> *'Personal challenge - the desire to communicate without the frustration of not being able to express myself'.*

We see then that visiting students come with a variety of motivations, but perhaps the overwhelming reason for coming to Britain on an exchange scheme is to improve their English, both because of a genuine interest in British people and culture and because of the practical advantages it will bring them in their studies and in their future careers.

Integration

Seven questions dealt with integration in Southampton, in particular who the students were living with, who their friends were, how easy or difficult they felt it was to make friends with British students, and what clubs and societies they had joined.

Seventeen of the respondents were living in a university hall of residence and the other two in private, shared houses. Sixteen of the students (84%) were sharing with British students. Thus, from this point of view, they were very well integrated.

The students were also asked to list the nationalities of their three best friends in Southampton and the results were tabulated as follows:

Table 3. Nationalities of Three Closest Friends in Southampton

	1st	*2nd*	*3rd*	*Total*
Same nationality	11	9	6	26
UK	6	4	6	16
Other European	2	5	4	11
Other non-European	-	1	1	2

Other European and other non-European in the table sometimes include the same native language, e.g. a German with a Swiss friend, or a Spaniard with a Mexican friend.

Four of the respondents (21%) listed more than one of their best friends as coming from the UK, while eight (42%) claimed that their three closest friends were all from outside the UK. All of the students reported some British friends although a majority (10) said that they accounted for 30% or less. Four students reported that 31-50% of their friends were British, three 51-70%, and one over 70%. This contrasts with an earlier study (Blue 1991) which found that over 20% of the non-Europeans and half of the South Asian and African students questioned felt that they had no British friends at all.

Fourteen of the respondents (74%) said that it was hard to make friends with British people. They made the following kinds of comments on the subject:

> *'hard except language students'*
>
> *'very difficult - English are quite serious and sometimes arrogant'*
>
> *'When I arrived it was difficult because of my English'.*

Conversely, three of the students said that making friends with the British was easy e.g.:

> *'Very easy to make friends in a sports club - the only problem is that most of them are at least three years younger than me'.*

The overall feeling was that 'freshers' were approachable, because they had not yet formed their groups of friends, but second and third year students already had their circles of friends and were not too interested in expanding them. As most of the visiting students are the equivalent of second or third year students, this means that they can most easily make friends with British students who are not on their courses and who are, most usually, younger than them.

When asked about their membership of clubs and societies, the respondents claimed to have joined a total of eighteen clubs between them, with only two students reporting that they had joined no clubs. The large number of clubs and societies mentioned suggests that this particular group of students is taking a very positive approach to integration and that they are taking an active part in the social and cultural life of the University.

Language Learning

This section dealt with the students' enrolment in classes and their experiences with language learning at Southampton, both within the context of the in-sessional classes offered by the Language Centre and in the wider context of their experience at the University of Southampton.

The students were asked whether they had enrolled in the in-sessional classes offered by the Language Centre and if so, which ones. Their responses broadly reflected the overall pattern of enrolments, shown in Table 4.

The students were also asked about their experiences with English and whether and what they had learned. They were asked to indicate the importance of certain activities in their present course of studies and to rate how they felt about their ability to cope with the language demands of each of these areas. The results are given (in descending order of perceived importance) in Table 5 and (in descending order of confidence) in Table 6.

Table 4. Total Enrolment of Visiting Students in In-Sessional Classes

Class	*Total*
Pronunciation	55
Grammar	55
English in the News	35
Proficiency	56
Academic Writing	59

Table 5. Perceived Importance of Activities to Respondents' Courses of Study

	Very important	*Quite important*	*Not important*
Reading books and journals	14	5	0
Writing essays, papers, etc	10	9	0
Listening to lectures	10	7	1
Doing practical work (lab, workshop, hospital, etc.)	10	3	4
Participating in seminars	8	3	8
Taking notes from lectures	7	8	4
Taking notes on books and journals	7	6	6
Receiving practical instructions (lab, etc.)	7	4	6
Attending individual supervisions and tutorials	3	4	10

Table 6. Respondents' Judgement of their Ability to Cope with Language Demands

	Confident	*OK*	*Unsure*
Understanding what you read in books and journals	11	8	0
Making adequate notes on what you read	11	8	0
Understanding lectures	10	8	1
Understanding instructions for practical work, etc	10	7	2
Discussing with your supervisor in individual supervisions	7	7	5
Taking adequate notes from lectures	7	6	6
Expressing your views and asking questions in seminars	1	6	12
Writing essays, papers, etc.	0	11	8

As might be expected, the students tended to be more confident in their receptive skills. The biggest mismatches between importance and ability were in 'writing essays' and in 'expressing your views'. These were seen as being important by the majority of the students, but only one student felt confident about expressing their views and none were confident about writing essays.

All of the students reported that their English had improved since October. A majority of the respondents (11) chose the category '*quite a lot*' and three reported that it had improved '*a great deal*', making a total of 74% in these two categories. Only five of the students (26%) said that their English had improved just '*a little*'. They were then asked to indicate what they felt had helped them to improve. Highest ranked (19) was '*talking and listening to native speakers on an informal basis*'. This was followed by '*attending lectures/ seminars/ supervisions in your department*' (15), '*listening to the radio, watching television, etc.*' (14), and '*talking and listening to other non-native speakers on an informal basis*' (11). '*Attending in-sessional English classes*' ranked fifth with only seven (37%) respondents claiming that they had helped. This is perhaps not surprising considering that only 28% claimed to have attended classes regularly! It is interesting to note though that the respondents appeared to feel that social interaction had helped their English more than formal learning situations.

In answer to the question of what, if anything, had prevented the students from improving their English, seven students (37%) reported that they had too much work for their main course of study, and six (32%) said that it was because of not making friends with native speakers. Eight of the respondents (42%) specified other factors such as:

> *'maybe this process takes longer than I want it to'*
>
> *'I sometimes was too lazy, should have read more books, should have used facilities at Language Centre'*
>
> *'too many French friends'*
>
> *'knowing too many Germans'*
>
> *'too many Italians around'*.

When asked to indicate what they wanted to learn about in in-sessional classes, the respondents ranked '*Everyday English*' highest with eighteen mentions (95%). This was followed by '*English society and culture*' with thirteen (68%), '*English for your future work*' with eleven (58%), and '*Preparation for English Exams*' with nine (47%). '*English related to your academic subject*' only received four mentions (21%) and '*Academic study skills*' came bottom with one. Thus academic skills rate relatively low on the students' list of priorities, although the professional aspect of '*English for your future work*' was considered to be quite important.

The final question the respondents were asked was about what other types of classes they would like to see offered by the Language Centre. Three of the respondents wanted classes aimed at British culture and society, presumably feeling that the present provision in this area was inadequate:

> *'English way of life, social conditions, the country'*
>
> *'Intercultural communication and how to understand the reactions and behaviour of English people, how to fill the gap of the different cultures'*
>
> *'English society, culture and history'*.

Two of the students commented on the size of the current classes rather than on their content or aims, and two wanted more grammar.

IMPLICATIONS FOR EAP TEACHING

On the basis of our limited survey it would seem that our decision to offer a separate programme of in-sessional classes to visiting students, one that has fewer academic and more general purpose English components, was justified. It would be interesting to follow this up with a more extensive study, perhaps involving other institutions. A future project could also be to carry out a similar study with *registered* EU students.

As a branch of ESP, it is generally considered that EAP will be 'goal directed' and 'based on a needs analysis, which aims to specify as closely as possible what exactly it is that students have to do through the medium of English' (Robinson 1991). This may involve a 'common core' approach to the teaching of EAP or it may involve teaching the discourse and conventions of a particular discipline. Even though practitioners are not agreed as to how specific EAP needs to be, most would agree with Hutchinson and Waters that ESP (and hence EAP) should be seen as 'an approach to language teaching which is directed by specific and apparent reasons for learning' (1987).

When we consider visiting European students, though, the goals and the needs are not always very easy to discern. We have seen in this study that the group of students in question were highly motivated to learn English, both for reasons of integration and for the academic and professional benefits that a good knowledge of English could bring them. We have also seen that they were quite well integrated with British students, participating fully in University life, and that they considered social interaction to be the major factor in improving their English. Although they considered expressing their views in seminars and academic writing to be the areas in which they were the least proficient, they wanted in-sessional English classes to focus on general purpose English (GPE) and English culture and society.

Thus, although there would seem to be a limited role for EAP classes focusing on the main study activities that students are involved in, these visiting students are certainly not interested in developing a narrow competence restricted to the academic domain. What Widdowson (1983) has claimed for EAP in general is certainly true for these visiting students: 'At this end of the scale, ESP shades into GPE'.

REFERENCES

Albert, T. (1976) 'If you were foreign.' Times Higher Education Supplement, 221

Blue, G.M. (1991) 'Language learning within academic constraints.' In Adams, P., B. Heaton, and P. Howarth (Eds.) *Socio-Cultural Issues in English for Academic Purposes*. London and Basingstoke: Macmillan

Department for Education (1994) *Statistical Bulletin 15/94: Students from abroad in Great Britain 1982 to 1992*. London: DFE

Gardner, R.C. and W.E. Lambert (1972) *Attitudes and Motivation in Second Language Learning*. Rowley, Mass.: Newbury House

Hutchinson, T. and A. Waters (1987) *English for Specific Purposes: A learning centred approach*. Cambridge: Cambridge University Press

Robinson, P.C. (1991) *ESP Today: A practitioner's guide*. Hemel Hempstead: Prentice Hall

Weir, C.J. (1983) *Identifying the Language Problems of Overseas Students in Tertiary Education in the UK*. Unpublished PhD Thesis, University of London Institute of Education

Widdowson, H.G. (1983) *Learning Purpose and Language Use*. Oxford: Oxford University Press.

PART TWO:

EAP AND ACADEMIC DISCOURSE AND GENRE

From the General to the Specific: What the EAP Tutor Should Hnow About Academic Discourse

Alan Lockett
University of Bristol, Language Centre

TENSION AND CONFLICT

The EAP class can sometimes seem beset by the duality of demands of specificity and generality. Perhaps the most familiar of EAP settings is that of the pre-sessional course where students from a variety of disciplines are grouped together with general academic skills and language providing the focus. On the face of it, this presents a scenario in which the more subject-specific language needs appear to be undermined. Yet the tension between the student's specificity of need and the "generalist" paradigm operative in many pre-sessional EAP classrooms need not lead to conflict. In fact, such conflicts as do arise in the EAP class would appear to me to be attributable, not so much to the absence of narrowly subject-specific content, but rather to unprincipled or ill-informed practice.

This paper argues that resolution is more likely to occur where there is a clear focus, informed rather than intuitive, on general academic discourse (hereinafter referred to as GAD) as a generative "common core". This will operate as an enabling resource, within what might be termed the transitional pedagogy of EAP, from which students of various disciplines may proceed to their own discoursal goals. The concern here is motivated by perception of the relative insufficiency of 'traditional' practice in academic writing tuition, and hence of the need for developing properly focused and well-founded procedures within EAP settings.

SOME ASPECTS OF SPECIFICITY AND GENERALISABILITY

Consideration of how best to address students' English language and study needs in relation to their subject areas involves us in examining the issue of specification. In addressing the notion of 'purpose', a narrow subject-content interpretation would see specificity as being challenged by the prevailing practice of multi-disciplinary groupings on pre-sessional EAP courses. Such an approach elevates subject matter to prime "homogenising" position in the pantheon of purpose. Some course directors have perhaps, either explicitly or implicitly, subscribed to such a view by operating broad subject-based splits of EAP students (e.g. Science/Technology v. Arts/Social Science) on pre-sessional programmes.

It is not that I would wish to suggest that this type of approach is necessarily unfruitful. However, much of the past research undertaken in the area of analysis of academic/technical texts (from frequency to register to functional/rhetorical analysis) is thought by many to have failed to indicate "substantial" linguistic differences to distinguish specific subject areas. The prevailing view is that a great deal of language is generalisable across subject boundaries (leaving aside here the issue of what linguistic-analytical basis this generalisability might be founded upon). This is not to ignore the more *genre*-based observations of such as Dudley-Evans (1993) and Johns (1988), who both draw attention to variations in communication patterns between discourse communities. We should indeed guard against the kind of blanket overgeneralisation Dudley-Evans (1993) warns against: '*...An approach to the teaching of academic writing that implies that there are common patterns of organisation that always apply in all disciplines...*' is not what is being advocated here.

A strong view of the implication of the generalisability of language across subject areas might appear to undermine specific/academic purposes teaching completely, and possibly even lead to the conclusion (arrived at by some detractors of ESP/EAP) that it might as well be abandoned as a distinct enterprise. Yet I believe there are valid reasons for resisting a retreat back into general purpose English, just as there are for resisting straining towards specificity of subject-content. The greater precision of specification implicit in EAP as an enterprise need not necessarily entail the abandonment of a generalist paradigm in mixed-discipline pre-sessional courses, but rather requires us to be clearer, indeed to be specific(!), about what and to what extent is in fact "general" or "generalisable". If writing components within pre-sessional EAP courses are in fact seen as operating on the basis of the construct of GAD, with subject-specificity being regarded as largely a matter of a disciplinary lexico-conceptual overlay (with perhaps a few field-specific "sub-generic" elements acquirable outside the EAP classroom context), then the construct ought to be made more explicit.

It should be borne in mind that an EAP course is, first and foremost, a "language" course, and the teaching of any "subject content" is, as it were, incidental to this. To put it another way, it is a course in which the focus is on the packaging of information rather than the information itself, in which, unlike prospective specialist content courses, the medium is very much the message. And what is most apparent about academic discourse would appear to be its predominant descriptive-analytical and interactive-informational dimensions across a range of disciplines, and it is this that goes to make up GAD . With this in mind, those frameworks of analysis and sources of information which highlight these aspects of discourse will be of particular relevance to EAP.

RESOLUTION: GAD AND WHAT THE EAP TUTOR SHOULD KNOW

It would appear to me that standards of writing teaching on EAP courses have sometimes suffered from being (mis)informed by somewhat facile notions and received pseudo-wisdoms concerning the nature of academic writing. The tendency towards reliance on superficial, intuitive or impressionistic notions which gloss the real nature of academic writing has, it must be said, to some extent been purveyed by the very textbooks/writing handbooks which purport to give students useful guidelines and insights into the writing process. This sense of the relative inadequacy of some of these "secondary sources" further underlines the need for consideration of more "primary" descriptive material. Recognition of the proper role of the EAP tutor, as a bridge between the students and their target situation requirements, means that EAP practitioners must concern themselves with raising their own awareness of academic discourse, as well as developing a coherent enabling pedagogy. With this in mind, the areas outlined here are seen as being of relevance to EAP tutors in enhancing the range of procedural tools in their repertoire for facilitating students' understanding and production of academic discourse.

The following sections seek to provide a few brief pointers towards areas of analysis and research work which seem to have potential for raising awareness of the workings of academic discourse across disciplines. Lest I lay myself open to the charge of insufficient rigour in failing to elaborate a detailed analytical model of the construct of GAD, I should state that this does not lie within the scope of this particular paper. Here I have set myself the more modest practical, informing, facilitatory brief of drawing together various potentially fruitful vantage points for the benefit of those recently inducted into EAP and seeking some signposts to help them along their way (see Table 1).

LINGUISTIC VARIATION: DIMENSIONS OF ACADEMIC PROSE

Biber (1988) aims to describe the textual relations among spoken and written genres, seeking to map the functional dimensions of language variation among texts and to provide an overall description of relations among genres with respect to these dimensions.

His approach, a multi-feature and multi-dimensional analysis, uses frequency counts of particular linguistic features, along the lines of traditional frequency and register analysis, the difference from these old approaches being that a "consistent co-occurence pattern among features" is sought. In his words, when a group of features consistently co-occur in texts, those features define a "linguistic dimension", the assumption being that strong co-occurrence patterns of linguistic features mark underlying functional differences. For example, the co-occurrence pattern between passives and nominalisations can be interpreted as representing an underlying abstract or informational focus, characteristic of academic prose in general.

Thus proceeding from the linguistic features that are in fact used systematically in texts to an account of the underlying functional dimensions of English will allow identification of the functional dimensions that are important enough to be systematically marked and the relative "coverage" of different discourse functions. Once linguistic dimensions are identified and interpreted, they can be used to specify the 'textual relations' among different kinds of texts in English. For EAP students, many of whom show themselves insufficiently aware of the key dimensions along which spoken and written genres vary, this would appear to have great potential. The somewhat fuzzy notion of "register", often invoked rather vaguely in explanations by EAP tutors, may become more fixable through the application of this kind of framework.

DISCOURSE AND TEXT ANALYSIS: THE BIRMINGHAM SCHOOL

A great deal of work has emerged in recent years from a number of scholars associated with the University of Birmingham. The scope of this outline does not permit a proper indication of the full extent and range of this work, but some broad lines may serve as a pointer to its relevance for EAP.

A suitable starting point would be with Winter (1976) and Hoey (1979, 1983), and their analysis of *text organisation*. According to this view, speakers and writers normally provide, and listeners and readers perceive, pattern(s) in text, which may be thought of as culturally popular patterns of organisation, describable in terms of semantic relationships between clauses and groups of clauses. Broadly, Hoey's work attempts to show how the functions of a particular discourse's constituent sentences are "signalled" linguistically. Typical patterns of organisation are discussed in Hoey (1983), who identifies a recursive rhetorical structure common in expository text - that of *Situation, Problem, Solution, Evaluation*. Applications

Table 1. GAD: Some key sources of information for the EAP writing tutor

Researcher(s)	*Research Area*	*Area of Focus for EAP writing pedagogy*
Biber	Distinctive linguistic features of academic prose	linguistic features of texts related to functions of discourse *key dimensions of academic prose: 'register"*
Francis	Discourse labelling	labelling function of nominal groups in discourse organisation *function of nominalisations in signalling transitions/topic management*
Hoey, Winter	Clause relations and text structure	semantic relations in inter- and intra-sentential structure linguistic signalling of functions in discourse rhetorical structure of expository text (e.g. Problem Solution pattern) lexical cohesion (coherence procedures) *paraphrasing: lexico-syntactic relations (subordination/connectors/lexical items)*
Hyland, etc.	Hedging in academic writing	reader-writer interaction: indicating of writer's position towards propositions *syntactic and lexical realisations of modality*
Myers, Bazerman	Social construction and 'rhetoric' of science	syntactic devices related to rhetorical purpose *rhetorical 'tricks': multiple embedding, nominalisations, lexicalisation*
Swales, Dudley Evans	Genre analysis	rhetorical choice related to authorial/communicative purpose typical information structuring in various genres (rhetorical 'moves in RP Introductions)' *linguistic features of rhetorical 'moves'*
Tadros	Prediction in text	lexico-syntactic features in rhetorical signalling (e.g. Enumeration, Advance labelling) *sub-technical and discourse reference nouns*
various	Composition and Rhetoric studies	procedural knowledge *cross-disciplinary discourse conventions*

and adaptations of some of Hoey's analytical procedures would seem particularly useful to the EAP reading/writing tutor as tools in the development of productive writing skills. It is apparent that problems in unsuccessful discourses can often be attributed to inadequate signalling. Hoey himself points to the important practical consequences his work has for the teaching of rhetorically-based "technical" writing.

Hoey (1991) also devotes an entire book to the area of lexical cohesion, which is shown to be the most important form of cohesive tie. Hoey observes that lexical cohesion is the only type of cohesion that regularly forms multiple relationships and thus is the dominant mode of creating coherence and texture. The implication of this for more targeted work in the EAP classroom on contextualised lexical expansion and exploration is apparent, as is the disproportionate attention given to other more obvious but less generative aspects of cohesion, such as "connectives".

In other work looking at the metalanguage of English, Winter (1977) shows that relationships between clauses can be signalled in one of 3 ways: by subordination, which he terms *Vocabulary 1,* by sentence connectors, which include conjuncts, which he terms *Vocabulary 2, and* by lexical items, which he terms *Vocabulary 3.* He notes that items from all 3 vocabularies can frequently be used to paraphrase each other; for example by -ing, thus and instrumental may all be used in clauses indicating the logical sequence relation of instrument.

As well as further pointing to the need for lexical sensitisation, Winter's work suggests ideas for better-informed work on paraphrasing. All too often, it seems, EAP students are advised to paraphrase in order to avoid plagiarism, but tutors, and authors of published materials, have not always been as helpful as they could in properly illustrating how this can be done. An approach to developing students' lexico-syntactic resources could usefully start from a consideration of such a linguistic-analytical framework.

Winter's and Hoey's works points to the importance of lexical signalling, which is developed from slightly different angles in the work of Tadros and Francis.

Tadros (1985, 1994) presents a model of discourse analysis based on the notion of *Prediction*, a term she uses to refer to a writer-reader interactional phenomenon; a prospective rhetorical device, overtly signalled in the text, which commits the writer at one point to a future discourse act. She produces a taxonomy of predictive categories, namely *Enumeration, Advance Labelling, Reporting, Recapitulation, Hypotheticality, Question*, with criteria for membership within each category consisting of certain lexico-syntactic conditions. The detail of this approach cannot be gone into here, but what is significant for the EAP writing tutor would appear to be the quite heavy dependence on lexical items, e.g. for *Enumerables*, what might be termed "sub-technical" nouns (e.g. aspects, reasons, advantages, etc. as distinct from men, women, children) as well as discourse reference nouns (e.g. examples, definitions, classifications). Tadros' approach clearly has practical pedagogical applications, emphasising as it does the interactional relationship between writer and reader in discourse, as manifested through the use of predictive categories, which her research shows to be common across a range of disciplines.

In related work, Francis (1986, 1994) looks at how nominal groups are used as advance or retrospective "labels" to connect and organise written discourse. Advance labels are seen as having "predictive and organising functions" which can be seen "in terms of the 3 Hallidayan metafunctions: ideational, interpersonal and textual" (Francis, 1994); they indicate how a subsequent stretch of discourse is to be interpreted, providing a "frame of reference within which the subsequent argument is developed". Retrospective labels have an important organisational function, signalling the transition to the next stage by "encapsulating or packaging it in a single nominalisation". She notes that labels have much in common with Widdowson's (1983) "procedural" vocabulary which structures and supports the more specific field-related vocabulary of academic texts. This has obvious relevance to a GAD-based approach, as advocated here, and the importance of these labels for what might be termed *topic management* in academic discourse is evident.

GENRE ANALYSIS

Genre analysis looks at the operation of language within a complete text, seeing the text as a system of features and choices, with selection being made according to authorial communicative purpose. Choice of rhetorical function in academic writing, for example, is determined by the author's purpose, which is itself a function of the wider academic culture to which s/he belongs.

The fullest elaboration of this approach in an academic context is in Swales (1990). Briefly, people writing in an academic context may be viewed as members of an *academic discourse community*, sharing common public goals, with particular mechanisms for intercommunication between members and with discoursal expectations leading to the development and use of distinctive text types.

In an EAP context, the importance of this work for development of greater rhetorical awareness is evident, as is the need for greater emphasis on the role of the text in the so-called "community" and a greater consideration of "academic culture". At the rhetorical level, Swales' analysis of the various "moves" that research writers in various disciplines employ in structuring an introduction has achieved wide currency within the field. However, the extensive lip service paid to this work has, it seems to me, not yet been adequately reflected in EAP practice, which seems to be still unduly attached to an older Study Skills tradition. Weissberg and Buker (1990) and Swales & Feak (1994) are, to my knowledge, the only "published" EAP materials drawing substantially on genre analysis findings, and are based on texts across a variety of disciplines, providing a great deal of useful practice, tying rhetorical aspects of information structuring to lower level linguistic features within the genre of the research article. Dudley-Evans (1986) has used Swalesian analysis and applied it to other sub-genres of research writing, with some particularly useful work on discussion sections of postgraduate dissertations.

This kind of analytical framework would appear to have great potential as a tool for the EAP writing practitioner, at the interface between course design/materials writing and pedagogical procedures, in attempting to inculcate in students the formal schemata (Carrell, 1983) necessary for the production of acceptable academic discourse. There have been doubts cast as to the generalisability of insights yielded by analysis of this nature, but a number of EAP practitioners have reported (personal communication) improvements in the quality of discoursal competence of students exposed in Reading/Writing classes to materials and procedures informed by this type of analysis.

COMPOSITION AND RHETORIC STUDIES

The term "Composition and rhetoric studies" is used here as a convenient label indicating a broad area of research interest rather than to identify a narrow area or particular analytical approach. This work has been almost entirely US-based since the courses in freshman composition and rhetoric around which much of the research is centred are a feature of the US college system. However, there are considerable insights for the EAP practitioner, particularly in the context of academic writing, to be gained from such research in a closely related area.

Researchers such as Berkenkotter, Huckin and Ackerman (1988) and Hare and Fitzsimmons (1991) seek to explore the complex relationship between writers' prior knowledge and how they use that knowledge to generate academic discourse. Hare & Fitzsimmons' findings, for example, are significant in that they suggest that mere participation in an "interpretive community" without explicit instruction in its ways of writing can enhance students' ability to write in that community. Their findings also suggest that "participation in one interpretive community can facilitate writing in another community, provided the communities share discourse conventions". Such research provides useful insights into the distinction between "content knowledge" and "procedural knowledge" and their roles in the writing process in academic settings. Berkenkotter et al's case study of a student in a rhetoric PhD programme illustrates that available knowledge can be transported via writing from one field to another. The student soon appropriated the content knowledge of the field of study, but initially carried over into his academic writing the procedural knowledge of his teaching and expressive writing communities. In other words, he drew upon his knowledge of particular discourse conventions.

Here we may recall the notion referred to earlier of the EAP course, based on GAD, dealing with procedural knowledge and the student's content knowledge spiralling around this. It will help to productivise tension and avoid conflict if it is made explicit to students that dealing with content knowledge different from their field is not irrelevant, since it is procedural knowledge which is central in the EAP course. One thing that is apparent is that EAP students will benefit from extensive exposure to models (of various types of conventional successful rhetorical organisation) with a view to enhancing "procedural knowledge". It may help if the EAP tutor can somehow turn the classroom into a "micro-academy", so to speak, with students adopting the role of apprentices in the academic community.

In tying this in with our argument about the nature of EAP course content, it must be noted, however, that writing researchers have reported conflicting views between English language tutors/lecturers and those from other disciplines on the centrality of content. The "English composition" position (see e.g. Flower 1987, Scardamalia & Bereiter 1982) is that the selection and presentation of content are secondary to rhetorical considerations in expert writing processes. However, Jolliffe & Brier (1988), studying writing in disciplines outside English and composition, spoke of the centrality of content in expert writing, noting that "[experts] write about those subjects that form part of what Toulmin calls the 'language' of their rational enterprise - the concepts and key terms participants in the field read and write about". In Johns' (1991) study of an ESL science student who found consistent difficulty dealing with the writing tasks in an English competency exam, the student maintained that his understanding of biology terms and their relationship to concepts in the discipline was more important to his success in his classes than his ability to organise his essay response. Thus it would perhaps be unwise to argue for an exclusively generalist EAP paradigm. Indeed I would not wish to do so. The EAP student's ultimate discoursal goals are not to be detached or postponed for the duration of the EAP course, but should, as it were, spiral around, feeding into and feeding off the GAD-founded core.

RHETORIC OF SCIENCE

Myers' (1994) work is closely related to the work of sociologists of science, and is thus primarily directed towards the critiquing and "demystification" of science, but it is also important for what it tells us about how we might train novice academic writers to produce certain effects in their writing.

In examining the nature of scientific writing, Bazerman (1984) reviews the advice traditionally given to writers of scientific articles, which emphasizes the removal of self from report, the need for objectivity and precision (with mathematics as model), the avoidance of 'flights of rhetorical fancy', and the necessity for claims to be supported with empirical, preferably experimental, evidence. The work of Bazerman, along with other sociologists of science, such as Latour and Woolgar (1979) and Gilbert and Mulkay (1984), cast doubt on the conventionally-accepted objectivity of scientific writing, arguing that the main goal of, for example, experimental reports is "persuasion" rather than mere exposition. The perlocutionary force, so to speak, of a scientific research paper is thus to persuade the academic community to accept the new knowledge claims and to adjust its network of consensual knowledge to accommodate those claims.

Myers (1994) examines the linguistic differences between scientific research articles and their popularisations, and distinguishes contrasting underlying narratives, which he characterises as the *narrative of science* (where the scientific activity and the development of the discipline, as opposed to the objects of study, are the focus of attention) and the *narrative of nature*. He comments on various linguistic aspects involved in what might be termed the encoding of this *narrative of science.* These include syntactic devices, whose sophistication of effect is striking when considered alongside the conventional "rules" for writing science. For example, the use of the passive voice in describing processes is shown to be rhetorical rather than mandatory; thus there is strategic use of the active to foreground the personal work of researchers against which the description of the technical work then proceeds in the passive. Also research articles tend to contain sentences with multiple embedding, that bring a number of clauses into the same sentence, asserting them at once, again a rhetorical "trick", while similar content would typically be conveyed in the popularisations with a series of simpler sentences. Popularisations thus contain unpacked clauses, and also "unpack the nominalised verbs that are characteristic of scientific writing". Analogous to this in the lexical area is the "encapsulation of a narrative in a term"; this process of *lexicalisation* "makes a process into an entity" (e.g., hybridisation, DNA fingerprint). Again there would appear to be useful material for the EAP writing tutor, highlighting the need to move away from over-generic vagueness and received "wisdoms" to substantive representations of actuality, driven by real data.

We might also see the considerable amount of research on "hedging" in academic writing as being highly relevant here. This is usefully reviewed by Hyland (1994), who further points to the need to consider "...interactional elements which supplement propositional information in the text and alert readers to the writer's opinion", rather than continuing to plough the sterile furrow of impersonality. He stresses the need for pedagogic materials to adequately address the use of markers of epistemic modality, i.e. "hedges". Hyland's survey of currently used EAP textbooks, in addition to drawing attention to their failure to provide sufficient sensitisation and practice in this area, gives some useful indications as to the syntactic and lexical realisations of "hedging", which the EAP tutor would find instructive.

CONCLUDING REMARKS

The intention of this paper is to draw attention to the need for the writing pedagogy of EAP and those involved in it to move away form over-reliance on pre-packaged pseudo-solutions to the complex area of writing for academic purposes. It is hoped that this selective and somewhat restricted review of some useful areas of theory, description and analysis will point the EAP tutor towards becoming at the same time more informed, more autonomous, and more faithful to target situation requirements with regard to their teaching of academic writing.

REFERENCES

Bazermann, C. (1984) Modern evolution of the experimental report in physics: spectroscopic articles in *Physical Review*, 1893-1980. *Social Studies in Science* 14:163-96

Berkenkotter, C., Huckin, T. & Ackerman, J. (1988) 'Conventions, conversations, and the writers: case study of a student in a rhetoric Ph.D. program'. *Research in the teaching of English*, 22(1): 9-44.

Biber, D. (1988) *Variation across speech and writing*. Cambridge: Cambridge University Press.

Carrell, P. (1983) 'Some issues in studying the role of schemata, or background knowledge, in second language comprehension'. *Reading in a Foreign Language* 1(2): 81-92.

Coulthard, M. (ed.) (1986) *Talking about text*. University of Birmingham: English Language Research.

Coulthard, M. (ed.) (1994) *Advances in written text analysis*. London: Routledge.

Dudley-Evans, T. (1986) 'Genre analysis: an investigation of the introduction and discussion sections of M.Sc. dissertations'. In M. Coulthard (ed.)(1986), 128-145.

Dudley-Evans, T. (1993) 'Variations in communication patterns between discourse communities'. In G. Blue (ed.) *Language learning and success: studying through English*, 141-147. London: Modern English Publications.

Flower, L. (1987) *The role of task representation in reading-to-write*. (Tech. Rep. No. 6). University of California, Berkeley: Center for the Study of Writing.

Francis, G. (1986) *Anaphoric nouns*. University of Birmingham: English Language Research.

Francis,G. (1994) 'Labelling discourse: an aspect of nominal-group lexical cohesion'. In M. Coulthard (ed.)(1994), 83-101.

Gilbert, N and Mulkay M. (1984) *Opening pandora's box: a sociological analysis of scientists' discourse*. Cambrige: Cambridge University Press.

Hare, V. & Fitzsimmons, D. (1991) 'The influence of interpretive communities on use of content and procedural knowledge in a writing task'. *Written Communication*, 8(3): 348-378

Hoey, M. (1979) *Signalling in discourse*. Birmingham: University of Birmingham.

Hoey, M. (1983) *On the surface of discourse*. London: Allen & Unwin

Hoey, M. (1991) *Patterns of lexis in text*. Oxford: Oxford University Press.

Hyland, K. (1994) 'Hedging in academic writing and EAP textbooks'. *English for Specific Purposes*, 13(3): 239-256.

Johns, A. (1988) 'The discourse communities dilemma: identifying transferable skills for the academic milieu'. *English for Specific Purposes*, 7(1): 55-59.

Johns, A. (1991) 'Interpreting an English competency examination'. *Written Communication*, 8(3): 379-401.

Jolliffe, D. & Brier, E. (1988) 'Studying writers' knowledge in academic disciplines'. In D. Jolliffe (ed.) *Writing in academic disciplines*, 35-88, NJ: Ablex.

Latour, B. and S. Woolgar. (1979) *Laboratory life: the social construction of scientific facts*. London: Sage.

Myers, G. (1994) 'Narratives of science and nature in popularizing molecular genetics'. In M. Coulthard (ed.)(1994), 179-190.

Scardamalia, M. & Bereiter, C. (1982) 'Assimilative processes in composition planning'. *Educational Psychologist*, 17, 165-171.

Swales, J. (1990) *Genre Analysis*. Cambridge: Cambridge University Press

Swales, J. & Feak, C. (1994) *Academic Writing for Graduate Students*. Michigan: University of Michigan Press

Tadros, A. (1985) *Prediction in text.* University of Birmingham: English Language Research.

Tadros, A. (1994) 'Predictive categories in expository text'. In M. Coulthard (ed.)(1994), 69-82.

Weissberg, R. and Buker, S. (1990) *Writing up research.* New Jersey: Prentice-Hall

Widdowson, H.G. (1983) *Learning purpose and language use*. Oxford: Oxford University Press.

Winter, E.O. (1976) 'Fundamentals of information structure: a pilot manual for further development according to student need'. mimeo, Hatfield Polytechnic

Winter, E.O. (1977) 'A clause-relational approach to English texts: a study of some predictive lexical items in written discourse'. *Instructional Science* (special issue) 6(1): 1-92.

Problematising the Language Problem

Joan Turner
Goldsmiths College, University of London

INTRODUCTION

The concern of this paper is basically to problematise the conceptualisation of language in the institutional discourse in which EAP (English for Academic Purposes) is located. In this discourse, in as much as it surfaces at all, language surfaces as a problem. When all is going well and the message is successfully delivered, 'language' is not noticed. However, when the message is not successfully delivered, or the 'appropriate' message is not even attempted, it is 'language' which needs 'remedial' attention. I want also to problematise this relationship between language and content in which language is the inferior partner, the one that can be improved or 'supported' in the service of content, which remains static, presumably as established knowledge. I will look at the issue briefly from three different angles: the culturally embedded conceptualisation of language as medium; the historical instantiation of EAP and its presuppositions; and the institutional underacknowledgement of the complexity of issues that current EAP is faced with.

THE CONDUIT METAPHOR

The apparent transparency of language, unproblematically mediating between ideas and their expression, is linked to the deeply rooted cultural conception of language in the western tradition that it represents a pre-existing reality, whether the external reality of physical objects or the internal reality of thought. According to Harris & Taylor (1989), this tradition was only broken when Saussure formulated his conception of langue as a 'series of phonetic differences matched with a series of conceptual differences.' While Saussure's structuralist emphasis on language as a system of differences internal to itself, i.e. autonomous, enabled the establishment of linguistics as a science, the everyday conception of language as a representational medium lives on. The pervasiveness of what Reddy (1979) has termed 'the conduit metaphor' in the metalanguage of communication attests to its currency. We 'put things into words', 'get ideas across,' 'transmit messages', and so on.

The unsuitability of this metaphor for how communication actually works is suggested by Reddy himself who puts forward what he terms a toolmaker's paradigm, which emphasises the need to expend energy in communication, to negotiate and re-negotiate a common understanding of what's going on, rather than to assume the kind of automatic success that is presupposed by the conduit metaphor.

This (mis)conceptualisation of language has also been addressed by linguists. Halliday (1978) explicitly rejects the conduit model and his 'social semiotic' model emphasises both the reflecting and shaping force of language in society. Carter and Nash (1990) stress that it is important not to regard language merely as a window onto something else. They modify the transparency of language conception, stating: 'It is a medium that is active in the transmission of the message.'

A more radical step is taken against the language as conduit conception by Harris (1981) who asserts that the notion of language itself is a myth. In his book entitled *The Language Myth* he refutes both what he calls the 'surrogationalist', that is the traditional, nomenclaturist view of language, and the telementational model of Saussure, which is predicated on the interlocutors being privy to the systemic differences encoded in the langue. He advocates an integrational model of language (and of linguistics). In this view, the co-temporality of language use and communicational or interactional behaviour generally is stressed. Language cannot be successfully abstracted from other behaviours that make up the context. This formulation is not unlike the way Gee (1990), citing numerous ethnographic studies, describes the embeddedness of literacy practices in 'ways of talking, interacting, thinking, valuing and believing'. The academic practices that EAP is dealing with might also profitably be seen in this light, in other words as being enacted within a long-standing value system of academic culture.

EAP AND THE INSTITUTIONAL CONTEXT

The raison d'etre for EAP is the fact that mother tongue speakers of languages other than English wish to undertake English medium instruction. This suggests that the instruction would be the same in any other language. That is, the conceptual content is extant, presumably as 'objective knowledge' and can be relayed or transferred in whatever language is appropriate.

Such an assumption may be related to what Harris (1987) calls the 'cryptographic psychology' of the early machine translators, which maintains that what is said in English can be, as it were, mechanically encoded into the native language of the L2 student, who then decodes and encodes into English when called upon to speak or write in that language. As Harris points out in a different context (1981), such an assumption of 'interlingual equivalence' is an effect of the cultural matrix within which the view of language has been formed. He states:

> *The embedding of language in cultural practices, beliefs and traditions of all kinds, which may differ widely from one society to another, makes it naive to suppose that mere alignment between words and objects affords a universal method for establishing interlingual equivalences. That is not to say that in all cases, such a method is bound to fail. The point is rather, that opting straight away for such a method itself reflects cultural practices, beliefs and traditions of a certain kind. It assumes the validity of a view of language which is itself embedded in a particular cultural matrix.* (Harris, 1981)

The conduit view of language combined with a universalist epistemology and a 'cryptographic psychology' appear to be the underlying assumptions on which EAP plays out its institutional role. Language and knowledge are seen to inhabit clearly defined spaces but the former should ideally be able to perfectly (and hence invisibly) represent the latter. The perennial issue in EAP as to how much content knowledge the language teacher needs is also predicated on this hierarchical division between language and content. While EAP lecturers themselves are aware of the complexity of skills involved in the manipulation of language to perform the varying tasks required of students, the mindset of language use matching content masks this complexity and the multiple variability of language use itself.

LANGUAGE AS A 'TECHNICAL' PROBLEM

The prevailing attitude of academics in the receiving departments of overseas students may be seen as that alluded to by Carter & Nash (1990) in their reference to courses in literature and communications, 'there is a tendency to look *past* language at the more 'important' ideas or content that a text contains'. This privileging of content means that all sorts of problems are simply written off as 'language problems' and therefore 'technically' solvable with attendance at a (any!) language class. Similar perceptions are at work on the part of students, who see themselves as students of x discipline, rather than as students of language. Students often underestimate the extent to which they have to apply themselves to language study in order to execute the kinds of performance required of them and indeed, the kinds of performance they themselves would like to give. This is particularly the case with very able students who have no doubts about their ability to perform in their own language. Even when these languages are genetically completely different from Indo-European languages, the 'cryptographic psychology' still appears to apply. I know of at least one student who changed his PhD supervisor because the first one was 'always correcting my grammar mistakes and not discussing my work'. This scenario encapsulates a number of different and 'hidden' issues in the language/content debate. On the one hand, it points up the student's underestimation of the academic value of grammatically correct English, an element in the meticulous attention to detail expected of scholarly work. It also exemplifies, from the supervisor's point of view, the difficulty of extracting meaning from text which has not been produced in familiar ways. On the other hand, it highlights the differing perspectives between language specialists and non-language specialists on the use of the term 'grammar'. As used by a non language specialist it is as likely to encompass rhetorical structuring, register, cohesion, and so on as well as concord, or morphology which the language teacher might more readily designate as non-grammatical features. This maximising use of the term therefore stands in direct contradiction to its role in language teaching which tends to emphasise the importance of meaning and its emergence in discourse, or text beyond the level of the sentence. While teaching 'language as discourse' does not ignore sentence level grammar, it does not prioritise it in the same way. A further problem arises with the notion of 'correcting' bad grammar. Many PhD supervisors, unlike the one in the above example, would not go to the trouble of correcting the student's grammar. This would be too time-consuming. The supervisor might not think of it as her/his job to 'proofread' the student's text. The negative implication of this for the role of the EAP lecturer however is that 'proofreading' on the one hand or 'teaching the rules of grammar' on the other are the institutionally expected tasks. This oversimplification, not to mention misperception, of the EAP lecturer's role, embodied also in the maximising use of the term 'grammar' has the effect of reducing the language problem to a technical problem. With this reduction, the expertise of EAP lecturers, for example in understanding what their students are saying despite the fact that their rhetorical structuring or their grammar is not 'English', is left unacknowledged.

A further instance of the technicising of language in the institutional discourse of higher education is the mechanistic treatment of the British Council UCLES IELTS test.

Students are required to reach a particular cut-off point which arbitrates on the likelihood of their ability to be able to study successfully in English. If they reach that point but are still found to have difficulties performing in their particular disciplines, the call goes out for the cut-off point to be raised. This attitude both overstates the value of the IELTS test and underplays the complexity of language use. Language is perceived to be a surface level problem, not a constitutive player in the enterprise of academic production.

IELTS gives a guide as to students' basic language study skills, i.e. the extent to which they can interpret the expositional structure of texts and the relationship between ideas, both in verbal text and between visually presented statistical data and verbal text, but cannot account for the disjuncture between the implicit assumptions and expectations of their own educational culture and the one they will encounter in Britain, nor can it assess students' preparedness for the language demands of specific genres, or their command of the lexical fields most likely to be encountered in their disciplines.

CHANGING THE FOCUS OF EAP

While some university pre-sessional courses do see their remit as preparing students for IELTS, many take a broader perspective. Doing a pre-sessional course, especially if it is at the intended university, is in any case an enhancement over taking the test in the home country, as familiarisation with the campus, the library in particular, and the general way of life in the locality, enables a gradual induction into a new cultural existence.

The question of addressing the specific language demands of degree programmes has been enhanced by a deeper understanding of genre analysis (e.g. Swales, 1990, Miller, 1984) showing the inter-relationship between genres as specific socio-cultural practices and their rhetorical structuring, and such insights can be introduced into EAP courses. This is likely to be most satisfactorily carried out in subject-specific in-sessional courses, where the in-sessional language content is based on a selection of lectures, essays, and texts from the course itself, but teaching on such in-sessional courses in turn provides the language unit with greater knowledge of course genres and vocabulary fields and can enable, all else being equal, a degree of feedback into pre-sessional course content also.

THE INTERCULTURAL DIMENSION

While it is conceivable that a university course taking place in different countries and different languages might draw on the same sources, it is most unlikely that it would be delivered in the same way. Differences in educational culture include for example the number of books expected to be read or assignments and types of assignments expected to be written in the duration of a module or option; differences in the extent to which the injunction to read a book(s) is explicitly made by a teacher or implicitly expected of the students by handing them a reading list; and differences in teaching and learning genres, e.g the importance of the seminar in British education as opposed to its absence in some higher educational cultures. The minutiae of such differences are likely to become apparent to EAP lecturers first and foremost, as even after they have left pre-sessional courses, for example, students continue to seek advice. One example is of students approaching their English language tutors whilst they are on their degree programmes, proffering long lists, and asking them to provide advice on: a) which essay to choose, and b) which books to read. This may be as much an expectation of more explicit instruction from a tutor (see example below) than a misapprehension of the necessary study skill of reading widely or it might be an underestimation of the cultural value attached to the notion of independent study and hence independence of choice, or it might be some combination of all three. A full panoply of such issues is likely to remain unpredictable, with individual tutors only becoming more aware of the possibility of recurring issues with experience. My point is that a richer understanding of such issues is likely to reside with the EAP lecturer than with others.

The apparent informality of British tutors can be deceptive as critical comments, appropriately couched, for the British context at least, in palliative language, pass the student by. The difference in interactional styles between British and East Asian tutors can be summed up in the words of a Korean post-graduate student: '*in the oriental tradition, teachers take care of the students - very straight - to give advice, or to instruct- they don't digress ... the British way is to say: oh it's very good idea ..., BUT ... in a way they digress, it's not straightforward*' (from a recorded focus group discussion).

The ability to negotiate such cultural differences is not simply achieved by having them stated, although the assumption must be that stating them at least builds awareness and helps students to explain their frustration or confusion when they encounter them.

THE INTRA-INTERCULTURAL DIMENSION

The cultural dimension of academic practices is not restricted to overseas students. There is increasing documentation of the conflicts of identity that students feel in academic writing (e.g. Ivanic & Roach, 1990, Ivanic, 1992, Clark, 1992, Lea, 1994) which seems a culture apart from their everyday lives. With increasing numbers of people being encouraged to take up higher education, the gap between so-called 'native' and 'non-native' speakers of English is narrowing into a continuum, one which highlights the culturally specific nature of higher education and its value system.

Inducting students into that value system in Gee's (op.cit.) formulation 'ways of talking, interacting, thinking, valuing and believing' cannot be done without also developing their awareness and understanding of language use. They need not only to be able to develop an argument, for example, but to be able to recognise and analyse an argument structure. This means teaching the functional metalanguage, 'claims' 'substantiation', 'exemplification', 'given and new information', and so on, along with the embodiment of the functions in language. This cannot perhaps always be done at lower levels for students beginning a foundation course, for example, but might solve the problem of re-cycling the skills of essay writing which students often perceive as repetition of something they know while teachers see it as something the students need to continue to develop. (This in itself might be seen as a particularly entangled problem of educational cultural differences). Such a class could be entitled argument analysis in preference to academic writing, in order to signal its difference. Differences in cross-cultural communication could be the focus of a class called cross-cultural communication, thereby bringing in a degree of reflexivity into the more programmatic structure of traditional EAP.

FROM STUDY SKILLS TO 'VALUE-ADDED' LANGUAGE EDUCATION

The role of reflexivity, and integration of international students' experience into the EAP curriculum, questions the primacy or the centrality of the study skills framework for pre-sessional and access or bridging courses. While such a framework was perhaps the best strategy at the outset of EAP in the sixties and seventies, often in developing countries where the demand was for English language study skills which would provide an entrance into English language academic texts, primarily in science and technology, it now appears somewhat outdated. The provision is now led by the need to cater for students studying in Britain, at both undergraduate and post-graduate levels and over the whole range of subjects that higher education offers. This is a demand not only of students but of the universities themselves as they become increasingly dependent on the fee income of international students. If EAP is to promote its expertise and understanding of the cultural environment of academic study in Britain, beyond the constraints of the IELTS test, it has to raise both its institutional profile and attempt to give a fuller specification of what is does and is attempting to do. This could be helped by market forces as English as a valuable commodity in the global economy is often seen as a 'value-added' spin-off of a degree in Britain. English language competence could in fact be an understated motivation for students studying in Britain, particularly in business studies and other market oriented pursuits. This in effect represents the reverse of the language-as- pre-requisite model, where language is relegated to an entrance requirement. In such a case, it makes sense for language education to be an integral part of a degree. This format exists to some extent, particularly in the 'new' universities, but should perhaps be more fully utilised, as it provides an opportunity for EAP to enhance its institutional status. A market argument (unfortunately) is likely to carry more weight than a meritorious one.

CHANGING THE METALANGUAGE OF EAP

While the finer tuning of EAP curricula is relatively easy, changing the institutional discourse is more problematic. However, EAP practitioners themselves could make a start by addressing their own metalanguage and the assumptions it embodies. To a certain extent, it colludes in its own institutional marginalisation. For example, the terminology of 'support' could be avoided. The 'support' class is a 'cinderella' class, put on at times which interfere least with 'mainstream' education. Its brief is effectively to 'mop up' the problems of academic literacy in a foreign language and culture, as invisibly as possible. While the role of the in-sessional class is undergoing change, with some institutions incorporating language classes into their degree programmes, and others tailoring in-sessional classes more specifically to disciplines, a hierarchy of 'support' and 'subject specialism' prevails.

This is of a piece with the institutional discourse locating EAP as a 'service' and effectively reducing the role of language to one of technical adjustment. This distribution of power and labour has also been supported from within applied linguistics. The following quote from Widdowson (1979) provides an example:

> *...the formal linguistic characteristics of these varieties or registers of English are only of interest as realisations of underlying concepts and communicative operations associated with particular areas of enquiry which go under the general name of science and technology. Scientific and technical English is thus represented not as a variety of English text but as a textualisation of a variety of discourse which is itself independent of any particular language and expressive of a secondary and universal culture which scientists and technologists acquire through education* (1979).

The underlying assumption that students are already endowed with the cognitive disposition of scientific and technical discourse chimes in its style of thinking with what Street (1984) has critiqued as the 'autonomous' model of literacy. This model proposes similar powers for literacy as Widdowson's '*variety of discourse*' - in its independence of any language - proposes for scientific or technological thinking. The only difference is in the direction of the route travelled between language and cognition. In the one case, it is from literacy to cognitive capacity, and in the other, from cognitive capacity to language.

Such a mechanistic relationship is reinforced by another institutional term used to denote the practice of EAP. It is 'language training'. This connotes a muscular reflex rather than a complex process of cognitive exertion and intercultural negotiation. In pedagogical discourse, it harks back to behaviourism and automated responses. The notion that students undergo a period of 'language training' before going on to the 'real' world of study denies the complexity of what studying in another educational and language culture entails. If EAP sees itself as an area of expertise, pivotally able to contribute to that process, it needs to develop a more relevant metalanguage, and promote it by use both professionally and institutionally.

The absence of a more appropriate metalanguage for EAP is in marked contrast to the impact research by sociologists of science and knowledge (e.g. Gilbert and Mulkay, 1984, Latour and Woolgar, 1978) has had on the taken-for-granted-ness of the assumption that science is objective. The role of language in 'shaping written knowledge' (Bazerman,1988) has also been acknowledged, but the scope and potential of EAP in its institutional context remains underresearched, underpromoted, and under acknowledged.

LANGUAGE AS DISCOURSE AND LANGUAGE IN ACADEMIC DISCOURSE

While EAP has been formed within a discourse which has separated language from content, it is clear that such a clear-cut division does not exist. A grammar-translation method which both the conduit model of language and the universalist assumptions of a scientific discourse most strongly suggests is neither feasible nor pedagogically desirable.

To the extent that language teaching is viewed as teaching language as discourse (McCarthy and Carter, 1994) then the pedagogical concerns of EAP, EFL and mother tongue English converge. However, in the institutional discourse of higher education, language is only visible because of its failure to live up to transparency. This simplistic conceptualisation of language has to be addressed and EAP has to develop and promote a metalanguage for its *de facto* increasingly important role in the institution in order both to problematise that conceptualisation and to have that role acknowledged.

REFERENCES

Bazerman, C. (1988) *Shaping Written Knowledge.* Madison: University of Wisconsin Press

Carter, R. and Nash (1990) *Seeing Through Language*, Basil Blackwell, London.

Clark, R. (1992) 'Principles and Practice of CLA in the Classroom' in Fairclough, N (ed) *Critical Language Awareness,* Longman, London & New York

Gee, James Paul (1990) *Social Linguistics and Literacies: Ideology in Discourses*. London, New York, Philadelphia, Falmer Press

Gilbert, G.N. and M. Mulkay (1984) *Opening Pandora's Box: A Sociological Analysis of Scientists' Discourse* Cambridge University Press, Cambridge.

Harris, R. (1981) *The Language Myth* London: Duckworth
Harris, R. (1987). *The Language Machine*. London: Duckworth
Harris, R. and Taylor, T. (1989) *Landmarks in Linguistic Thought. The Western Tradition from Socrates to Saussure* Routledge, London, New York
Ivanic, R. and D. Roach (1990) 'Academic writing, power and disguise' in British Studies in Applied Linguistics, 5: Language and Power. Cilt, London.
Ivanic, R. (1992) "'I' is for Interpersonal: the discoursal construction of writer identities", Centre for Language in Social Life; Lancaster no. 42
Latour, B. and S. Woolgar (1979) *Laboratory Life: The Social Construction of Scientific Facts*, Beverley Hills, Calif: Sage
Lea, M. (1994) 'I thought I could write until I came here': Student writing in Higher Education,, in G. Gibbs (ed.) *Improving Student Learning: Theory and Practice* Oxford: OSCD
McCarthy, M. and Carter, R. (1994) *Language as Discourse. Perspectives for Language Teaching,* Longman, London & New York
Miller, C.R. (1984) Genre as Social Action. In *Quarterly Journal of Speech* 70: 151-67
Reddy, M. (1979) 'The Conduit Metaphor' in Ortony, A (ed) *Metaphor & Thought*, Cambridge, Cambridge University Press.
Street, B.V. (1984) *Literacy in Theory and Practice* Cambridge: Cambridge University Press
Swales, J. (1990) *Genre Analysis: English in Academic and Research Settings*, Cambridge University Press, Cambridge.
Widdowson, H. (1979) *Explorations in Applied Linguistics.* Oxford: Oxford University Press

Negotiating Academic Genres: The Double Burden for International Students

Jane Clarke
Department of Adult Education, University of Leicester

Carol Saunders
Division of Learning Development, De Montfort University, Leicester

Negotiating academic genres is not a new phenomenon, but it is an increasing requirement. Power and control of the higher education curriculum are located within academic disciplines and for students to be successful within the academy they must acquire the ways of knowing that are discipline specific. This has a significance for all students but creates a double burden for international students who are acquiring academic discourses in a second language.

This paper begins to explore the issues of cognitive mapping for students on multidisciplinary programmes in the current context of higher education. It suggests that there may be tensions between the patterns of curriculum development, student expectations and student assessment. A case study is used to illustrate the ways in which the problematic between disciplines may emerge and will focus on the relationship between language and cognition.

There is some indication that similarities exist in the ways that all students, whether writing in their first or second language, attempt to access academic discourses in parallel and may adopt strategies that have been put forward from within interlanguage theory. The challenge for universities is to empower students to overcome these obstacles.

INTRODUCTION

This paper focuses on the challenges for international students when they are faced with both working in a second language and accessing the variety of discourses required when they engage in multidisciplinary programmes. Here, to illustrate work in progress, we use a case study to identify how students import one disciplinary discourse into another in a similar fashion to the way in which they might import the rules of their first language into a second.

CONTEXT

The moves to mass higher education impact on the student experience in a number of ways. The growth in the proportion of 18/19 year olds in full-time higher education (13% in 1979 compared with over 30% in 1993), plus the increase in adult learners, in both full and part-time mode, has created a more heterogeneous student population. Added to this is the increase in international students. There are now over 100,000 full time international students in further and higher education in Britain (Education Statistics for the United Kingdom 1994). This mixed student population is being accommodated by a more diverse set of providers as further education colleges take on a greater proportion of undergraduate work.

For many the traditional experience of single subject (or joint) linear programmes has given way to curriculum delivery which is modular, semesterised and multidisciplinary, drawing on new academic disciplines or regions. The latter term being used by Bernstein (1990) to describe:

> *...a recontextualising of disciplines into larger units which operate in both the intellectual field of disciplines and in the field of practice. Regions are the interface between disciplines and the technologies they make possible.*

Regions might include, for example, 'Deaf Studies' or 'Media Studies' where students are unlikely to have had experience of the subject matter before embarking on their undergraduate programme. Students now grapple with several disciplines or regions concurrently and as a consequence need to manage a range of academic selves in parallel.

Not only is the curriculum differently packaged but it is also differently assessed. The pressures of modularity leave little time for diagnostic assessment with the result that most assessment is summative and consequently the impact of feedback is lessened.

These changes in the student population and delivery modes need to be contextualised in a situation of diminishing resources. This includes both human resources, as the staff-student ratio worsens, and learning resources, as library and support services experience increased demand (Wisdom and Gibbs, 1994). The pressures on higher education institutions to recruit international students are now greater than in the past and for these students there is the double burden of accessing academic discourses in a second language.

DISCOURSE, POWER AND INTERLANGUAGE

International students are faced with a number of challenges as participants in higher education in the UK. Firstly, they need to negotiate the target language, which is already familiar to the indigenous population. Secondly, they may need to access more than one target discourse if they are taking a joint or modular degree. Additionally they may be faced with a different organisational culture, and a different culture in wider society, to the one with which they are familiar. Although some of these issues would have been there in the past, there are now more international students and fewer staff to deal with them. The number of full time international students in higher education has increased from 49,800 in 1979 to 95,900 in 1993 (Education Statistics for the United Kingdom 1994).

Many universities have developed language centres to support these students and it is important to consider whether these are integrated within mainstream departments or are on the periphery. Since power and control of the higher education curriculum are located within academic disciplines, the centrality or marginality of such centres will affect their capability to empower students in the appropriate academic discourse.

Multidisciplinarity is a feature of universities offering joint degrees or modular programmes. Whilst disciplines are developing along separate and parallel tracks they are maintaining their distinctions and autonomy but not facilitating moves to interdisciplinarity.

Fish (1994) in stating the view of proponents of radical pedagogy, highlights the factors maintaining disciplinary separateness thus:

> *At the heart of that argument is the assumption that the lines currently demarcating one field of study from another are not natural but constructed by interested parties who have a stake in preserving the boundaries that sustain their claims to authority. The structure of the university and the curriculum is a political achievement that is always in the business of denying its origins in a repressive agenda. Knowledge is frozen in a form supportive of the status quo, and this ideological hardening of the arteries is abetted by a cognitive map in which disciplines are represented as distinct, autonomous, and Platonic.*

The failure of communication between disciplines, is noted as Fish (ibid.) continues:

> *Once knowledge has been compartmentalized, the complaint continues, the energy of intellectuals is spent within the spaces provided by a superstructure that is never critically examined.*

Whilst some regions are developing in ways which may challenge the status quo, the more established disciplines such as history, politics, sociology and psychology are like symbolic fortresses with their own hidden rules. There is little attempt by the academic community to communicate across disciplines, to find out what students need to know, and to develop interdisciplinary strategies. The new context of higher education makes it less likely that students get formative feedback on their work, which is difficult for all students. International students face the additional problem of not knowing whether they have hit the target language let alone the target discourse. This process is further complicated by the existence of a number of genre in a subject discourse. To take an area such as psychology, genre will vary according to the branch of the discipline: neuropsychology or social psychology, and according to the relationship between producer and audience. For example, an academic article where communication is between professional psychologists differs from a radio phone-in between psychologists and listeners.

Our research has focused on how students are accessing the ways of knowing in a discipline and presenting these through written assignments. Using case studies of writing in sociology, we have looked at students who are making the transition to sociological discourse. We are drawing on Selinker's (1972; 1992) theory of interlanguage to help us to understand the processes involved for students when they attempt to access the target discourse. It is important to bear in mind the complexity of this process for international students who are trying to access both the target language and one or two target discourses. Interlanguage is an approximate system; it is a manifestation of patterns of systematic errors. These patterns form an interlanguage and there may be several interlanguages as students process language into a target discourse. International students may be making systematic linguistic errors as they are progressing towards the target language of English; these may be overlaid by systematic discourse errors as they are accessing the target discipline discourse. These two processes will be occurring concurrently.

What generates these errors, which have become part of the student's learning process? Students have different learning strategies. They may, for example, draw on text book material from both disciplines without realising that within the social sciences there is more than one discourse. One result of failing to recognise this is that they over-generalise and draw material from one discipline into another inappropriately. For example, a student studying both sociology and psychology would deal with questionnaires in both disciplines. If, however, the student writing a sociology essay draws material on questionnaires from a psychology text they may fail to hit the target discourse; the subject matter is the same but the ways of dealing with it differ between discourses. If the student does not target the discourse accurately, systematic errors may emerge that are penalised and in this case the influence of one discourse on another will have negative consequences for the student.

However, the influences may also be positive and creative. Students may import ideas from one discipline to another in imaginative ways. There are parallels here with language. Words like the German 'verstehen', meaning empathetic understanding, are imported into sociology since there is no single English word with the same meaning. Integrating material from different disciplines can be very productive but can be problematic for students who are operating in an academic culture where knowledge is compartmentalized.

CASE STUDY

The following case study gives two examples to illustrate the complexity of the process. In both instances the student imports the discipline of psychology into her sociological research. The result may be an inappropriate target discourse or creative interdisciplinarity depending on whether the rules of the discipline are broken and on the judgement of the lecturer assessing the work.

Anita is a mature student studying sociology and psychology, who plans to specialise in psychology. She is a relative newcomer to both disciplines. Prior to writing up her sociology report, Anita had undertaken some psychology experiments. The focus of her research is gender relations in a primary school and she spent some time in a school to gather the data.

Anita writing up a sociological research report : Extract 1

> The problems associated with participant observation were held constant in the **experimenter's** mind in order to help alleviate the problems, however the participant observation was still subjective as it was only the **experimenter's** interpretation of the situation and experience that were reproduced in this report. There was also the problem of defining the **objective** of the study before the research began. The **experimenter was predisposed to the objective of the study** and it may be said that the **experimenter** was only observing information or situations that were relevant to the experiment Thus is may be said that the evidence was found to **prove or disprove the hypothesis**. It was hoped that the **experimenter** entered the **experiment** with an open mind in order to observe actions within the context of the situation.
>
> [Emphasis added]

Anita was using the method of participant observation. In sociology this means that the researcher observes in an empathetic way, trying to see the world from the point of view of those being observed. However in the rest of the text there are examples of the ways in which her linguistic confusion is a reflection of her cognitive confusion (Widdowson, 1979). The words she uses are inappropriate for the method she says she is trying to use. When she uses the term 'experimenter' this is a manifestation of her confusion as she is not doing an experiment, by controlling variables, but is trying to see the world from the point of view of the school children. This involves studying the world in as natural a way as possible without disturbing the situation. There are further examples of her cognitive confusion. Whilst ethnographic researchers using participant observation will have some ideas of what they might find through observation they are unlikely to identify one 'objective of the study'. They may have several objectives and are prepared to elicit the unexpected. The phrase 'to prove and disprove the hypothesis' is more common in positivist sociology and is redolent of natural science where you might, for example, hypothesise that plants are phototropic i.e. grow towards the light, and set up an experiment to prove or disprove it. In participant observation there are so many factors under scrutiny that a researcher might accumulate evidence which demonstrates that certain things are going on but you would not expect to prove or disprove anything.

This is an example of the way that the student has imported psychology into sociology inappropriately. The resulting interlanguage is not acceptable to sociology tutors. In the event, because she acted on formative feedback, Anita revised the piece and did very well. However, if this had not occurred, perhaps because it was handed in at the end of the module, she would have been penalised for inconsistencies and for using a psychological framework instead of a sociological one.

In the second extract the pattern of discourse influence is somewhat different.

Anita writing up a sociological research report : Extract 2

> As young children and the reaction of the teachers to the children was being studied, it was not possible to produce a structured questionnaire to research the hypothesis. Piaget pointed out that children up to the age of approximately 11 years were still undergoing cognitive development. He pointed out that the cognitive structures of 4-5 year olds are not similar to those of adults. Thus the answers to formal questions may produce a variety of alternative answers that represent the cognitive development of the child rather than the formal operational stage that adults predominantly act upon. Therefore a structured questionnaire of a macro study would appear inappropriate.

Here Anita is drawing on her psychological knowledge, in this case Piaget, to evaluate the appropriateness of using questionnaires with young children in her sociological research. The issue here is one of audience evaluation. Would Anita be rewarded or penalised for this creative interdisciplinarity? This may depend on the discipline through which the work is assessed or the particular view of the assessor. If this were presented as an education assignment, we would expect a positive response as the region of education draws on a number of disciplines. However, if it is presented to a sociologist it may depend on whether the individual concerned believes that the discipline should keep discrete discourse boundaries or should be permeating boundaries in the interests of interdisciplinarity. In any event this is a high risk strategy for students if the rules about what is permitted and prevented are not applied consistently. If this is confusing for indigenous students it must create an additional burden for international students.

How then can we empower students to access discourses in this new context of British higher education?

PEDAGOGICAL IMPLICATIONS

It is clear that tutors need to clarify what they expect from their students and that they need to convey this accurately. Ballard and Clanchy (1988) make this point succinctly:

> *... making the intellectual culture explicit for new learners is the best way of helping them effect a successful integration into it.*

Those who operate within discourse communities, including academic staff, do operate on the basis of agreed conventions, shared language, common goals and so on, which set the discoursal boundaries. However, when we try to clarify this for students a number of contradictions and complexities emerge creating barriers to this explicitness. In her recent research Stockton (1995) outlines the tensions in this process for history students. Her findings suggest that whilst tutors indicate that they expect students to have facility with argument, their marking practices suggest that they reward narrative:

> *The explicit definition of writing in history is 'argumentation'; the implicit expectation, however, is for narrative.*

While students are aiming for the explicitly defined target there is another covert target which is being sought by assessing tutors. This has implications for all students but for those on multidisciplinary programmes the messages will be mediated by a range of discourse experiences. Stockton (1995) found, for example, that students taking English and history courses imported ideas about argument and criticism from English into history. As a result this tended to break up the narrative and these students did less well in their assessments. Indeed the disparity in their grades between English and history was noted thus:

> *It should not be surprising to learn, then, that one factor that came up again and again in the sets of papers that were examined for this study was the remarkably low grades that upper-level English majors earned on a regular basis in history courses. English majors, particularly at the junior and senior levels, resisted writing as emplotment, and faculty responded accordingly.*

Stockton (1995) highlights the tensions between the two disciplines, when she focuses on one student's writing, by saying:

> *... the writer gradually began to rely on narrative primary sources for the chronological arrangement of her own story (and earned higher grades), but even in those cases, the instructor's comments revealed a discomfort with the specificity and dominance of the student's argument.*

Not only is the student misreading the discoursal cues by importing the rules for English into history (creating an interlanguage which is not highly regarded by the target discourse), but she is also receiving contradictory messages from the history staff who would claim to prioritise argument over narrative but, in fact, do exactly the opposite.

In the case of Anita (Extract 1) to which we referred earlier, she was able to respond appropriately to the feedback given and hit the target discourse of sociology when she redrafted. However, there is now considerable evidence (Hounsell, 1984; Lea, 1994) that students do not read feedback in the way that tutors expect. Indeed as one of our student respondents says:

> *The tutors say 'analyse' but you don't really know what they mean.*

On a multidisciplinary programme this will have a different meaning according to the discourse of a particular discipline. On a modularised, semester programme formative feedback, even of this limited type, is increasingly rare.

Some researchers are arguing for an empowering strategy that emphasises the similarities across academic discourse communities (Flower, 1990). The current thrust in UK universities is to support transferable skills programmes and many Enterprise Learning Initiatives take this generic approach. Other research (Hounsell, 1984; Stockton, 1995) suggests that students need to be able to recognise and utilise discipline-specific skills and methodologies if they are to be successful academically.

Our research, which draws heavily on Hounsell's (1984) work, is leading us towards a model in which subject teams need to clarify discipline-specific skills and methodologies. The model, which is still at a formative stage, would focus on a number of factors including the role of academic subject literature, argument, criticism, interpretation and evidence and try to strand out for students those areas that are distinctive to the discipline. Students need to be cognisant of the actual, not perceived, practices of the discipline if they are to act on the guidance given (Stockton, 1995). This model may have interdisciplinary implications although this would involve substantial challenges to the existing power structure of higher education.

Some examples here will help to show that students need to be clear about discipline codes if they are to be empowered. Hounsell (1984), comparing essay writing in history and psychology, shows that to be successful in history students need to use the subject literature to develop 'viewpoint' in which they link evidence to their argument (this overarching viewpoint may encompass what Stockton defines as the prevalence of narrative). By contrast in psychology, argument is less central as students are required to integrate their ideas with a consolidated view of the subject literature (Hounsell calls this 'cogency'). The position of evidence in psychology is also somewhat different to that in history. In psychology there is 'conceptual anchorage' (Hounsell, 1984) between the evidence and the theoretical frameworks as outlined in the literature. Thus, if students receive feedback in which they are asked to 'use the literature more effectively' they need to contextualise this in the particular discipline in which they are operating. In addition the role of criticism is very different in English compared with sociology; in the latter discipline it is more akin to evaluation.

Although Hounsell's (1984) research did not focus on multidisciplinarity, his findings have implications for our work. The concept of interpretation is pivotal to his analysis, since in both history and psychology it defines that which is 'individually distinctive' (1984). He goes on to say that this is exemplified in students where essays are written with the sources that have been tracked down rather than merely from them.

Interpretation can have other implications for the multidisciplinary student since their capacity to put their individual 'stamp' on material may mean, as in Anita's case, that one discipline influences another. This interdisciplinary positioning may be perceived in different ways by different sectors of the academy. Such challenges could provide opportunities for a creative and interdisciplinary dialectic. However, without support the majority of international students will find these challenges impossible to meet. Where international students need language support institutions must recognise that both generic and discipline specific skills have to be developed. In order for this to occur collaboration between subject teams and language centre specialists is essential.

NOTE

This article has emerged as a result of research undertaken by the authors and by Michael Clarke at Nottingham University. It is written in the spirit of its topic by a multidisciplinary team striving for interdisciplinarity! We have backgrounds in applied linguistics, education and sociology.

REFERENCES

Ballard, B. and Clanchy, J. (1988), Literacy in the university: an anthropological approach in Taylor, G. *et al Literacy by degrees*, Milton Keynes and Philadelphia, SRHE/OU Press, pp.7-23.

Bernstein, B. (1990), *The structuring of pedagogic discourse: class, codes and control. Vol.4*, London and New York, Routledge.

Fish, S. (1994), *There's no such thing as free speech*, New York and Oxford, Oxford University Press.

Flower, L. *et al* (1990) *Reading-to-write*, New York and Oxford, Oxford University Press.

Hounsell, D. (1984), *Student's conceptions of essay writing*, unpublished PhD, University of Lancaster.

Kress, G. (1993), Genre as social process in Cope, B. and Kalantzis, M. (eds.), *The power of literacy: a genre approach to the teaching of writing*, London, Falmer Press.

Lea, M. (1994), "I thought I could write until I came here": student writing in higher education in Gibbs, G. (ed.), *Improving student learning: theory and practice*, Oxford, Oxonian Press, pp.216-226.

Selinker, L. (1972), Interlanguage, *International Review of Applied Linguistics*, Vol.X, No.3.

Selinker, L. (1992), *Rediscovering interlanguage*, London, Longman.

Stockton, S. (1995), Writing in history: narrating the subject of time, *Written_Communication*, Vol.12, No.1, January, pp.47-73.

Widdowson, H.G. (1979), *Explorations in applied linguistics*, Oxford, Oxford University Press.

Wisdom, J. and Gibbs, G. (1994), *Course design for resource based learning: Humanities*, Oxford Centre for Staff Development.

The authors wish to acknowledge the support they have received from the Academic Literacy Research and Interest Group coordinated by Mary Scott at the Institute of Education in London.

Teaching Socio-Professional Discourse: A Needs-Analysis Approach

Brenda P. Imber and Maria G. Parker
English Language Institute, University of Michigan

INTRODUCTION

The number of international students studying at US universities continues to expand. With this increase has come a growing awareness of the role these students play in the academic community. Swales (1993) notes that international Ph.D. students in the US are expected to "[engage] in a full range of main-stream academic activities," and Huckin & Olsen (1991) address similar requirements of non-native speaker (NNS) graduate engineering students. To date, however, the complexity of the relationships between student and university expectations has received little attention.

While graduate academic discourse communities may share base-line language proficiency expectations, different departments and/or programs have varying expectation levels of socio-professional discourse competence. From an institutional perspective, these variations affect EAP course content, methodology and instructional goals. From the NNSs' perspective, the variations can mean the difference between minimal or no language instruction to instruction for near native speaker (NS) proficiency level. This paper focuses on determining student expectations and on how one might construct a manageable approach to meeting those expectations in one typical academic discourse community - the MSc engineering programs at the University of Michigan.

RESEARCH

We conducted a preliminary case study of the oral discourse needs of international students pursuing the Master of Science in engineering (MSc) at the University of Michigan. The students in this program were chosen for the initial research because they constitute the largest number of foreign students at the University.

The initial investigative purpose was to gain a qualitative impression of the ESL[1]/ESP needs of the MSc's in their academic discourse communities, specifically the issue of student realities and oral fluency needs. The goal was to determine what students perceived as the greatest gaps in their English.

---

[1] ESL (English as a second lanuage) is American usage. It equates with EFL (English as a foreign language) as used by UK practitioners.

An informal unstructured interview format was used in order to elicit the greatest range and depth of responses and issues. The interviews were loosely anchored to the following questions:

1. What are your department's expectations of you as an international graduate student?
2. What fluency gaps do you now recognise you have and what's your wish list for courses to help you?

PRELIMINARY FINDINGS

In responding to the first question, MSc's reported that before coming to the US they expected that:

1. acceptance to the university graduate program implied acceptance of their English proficiency level; i.e. since they had met the TOEFL score requirement they had demonstrated a proficiency level sufficient for successful completion of their graduate work at our university; and that
2. simply by virtue of being in an English speaking environment, their fluency would improve in proportion to their specific needs.

What they find, however, runs contrary to their expectations. First, in the academic environment, the international MSc's find they are expected to:

- devote themselves to achieving excellence in research;
- provide research assistance and collaboration;
- help prepare professional publications;
- develop the ability to co-present papers at scientific conferences; and
- serve as graders, lab assistants/instructors, and in some cases become teaching assistants.

In addition to these academic realities, there are also significant socio-cultural realities which have emerged. The students all perceive a specific kind of fluency gap, namely, the need for a more comprehensive type of competence which can best be described as fluency in the socio-professional discourse register. By this is meant the discourse that contains a blend of professional and social register elements such as the co-mingling of social and professional collocations and idioms used when "chit-chatting" within a professional setting, the kind of semi-formal shop-talk that goes on in study groups, informal committee meetings, or the interchange between a speaker and an audience member.

All the respondents cited a critical need for instruction in this *blended* register in order to communicate and interact more effectively in situations that require fluency in socio-professional discourse. However, exploration of the everyday reality of their lives reveals that:

- the MSc's are in engineering classes that do not require much group work. Thus, there is little external structure that would initiate or encourage collegial contact.
- The MSc's live largely in what may be termed an Asian microcosm - large apartment complexes that are predominantly occupied by others like themselves, namely, Asian

MSc's. These residences are the most convenient to their classes and research labs as well as the most economical places for them to live.
- Their financial status also impacts on their ability to integrate socio-culturally. MSc's' social lives appear to consist mainly of activities among themselves, and if married, with their spouses/young children. There are Chinese and Korean owned markets nearby where they do their daily shopping (and where NSs need interpreters), and their free time (if they perceive that they have any) is spent navigating a very large store that covers all their needs and carries many types of Asian produce.
- MSc students are usually exposed to US culture for the first time.

These socio-cultural differences result in a rather limited need-to-use basis for English. Overall, most MScs have very little time, money or motivation for integrating with the NS socio-cultural life. Yet, despite these findings, our respondents continually stressed that the type of ESL courses they most wanted and needed contained instructional content that would improve their ability in socio-professional discourse.

RECOMMENDATIONS

Clearly, this informal interview phase of our analysis disclosed a need that is not being met adequately, if at all. Uncovering this gap raises the question of how EAP/ESP practitioners can respond to students' need for increased fluency in socio-professional situations.

As noted above, socio-professional interactions contain both professional and social components, thereby requiring the interlocutors to co-mingle various speaking and listening styles. Furthermore, this co-mingling is influenced by the shifting dynamics of the interactions themselves, making the language content and structure less than highly predictable. This lack of predictability, however, need not rule out helping students communicate more effectively and become more interactive and comfortable in such situations. While socio-professional events are not highly predictable, neither are they totally amorphous. They do have structures and components that can be identified and learned.

From our perspective, one of the most manageable methods for teaching socio-professional discourse is to use an integrative hierarchical approach, proceeding in steps of increasing specificity. This approach will be illustrated through a description of the steps in the following set of classroom activities.

PEDAGOGY

The needs analysis, previously described , identified a gap - a lack of fluency control in socio-professional situations. This leads to the first classroom step: students are asked to identify socio-professional situations they encounter. Once the issue of such situations is raised, most students are able and more than willing to discuss specific examples of situations they feel unequipped to deal with. Some of the most frequently mentioned situations are working on a group project or an informal committee, an office birthday party or other celebration, conversation with colleagues while waiting for a meeting to begin, small talk with a superior before getting to a delicate issue such as a salary raise, or a TGIF (Thank God it's Friday) (going out in a group for drinks) - although of course the specifics may vary according to student population. From the list of situations, one is selected for closer attention. Here the TGIF will be used, as it is a relatively universal event and often singled out by students as being especially difficult.

This point marks the transition from the first step to the second. From deciding on a specific situation the class moves to identifying and listing distinctive characteristics of that situation. At this point, the instructor and students list various components they expect to find in the chosen situation. To provide some structure to this activity, a worksheet such as the one shown in Figure 1 can be used. The left column identifies the general situation and the middle column is used to break down the situation into more discrete elements. For example:

At a TGIF there is a group of people plus bar staff, so interruptions are a typical component of the event. Figure 1 lists some of them:

- interrupting a professor or superior to order a drink;
- greeting a professor in a distinctly non-academic setting;
- deciding who pays;
- refusing alcohol.

Figure 1 *The Socio-Professional Situation*

LEVEL 1	LEVEL 2	LEVEL 3
EVENT TGIF (*Happy Hour*)	COMPONENTS ● MANAGING INTERRUPTIONS What if you're talking with a prof? ● GREETINGS How do you greet professors/advisors? ● PAYING / TIPPING / LEAVING Who pays? What if you leave early? ● REFUSING ALCOHOLIC DRINKS How do you say no? [ADD SOME OF YOUR OWN.] ● ● ● ●	LANGUAGE FOCUS

Adapted by Imber/Parker from Ellis & Johnson.
Teaching Business English. Oxford, 1994

Staying in this column, it is useful at this point to move from the general to the more specific - from a listing of components to some of their sub-elements. Note that even here the more that can be elicited from the students themselves, the more relevant the subsequent language activity will be.

Examples are shown in Figure 2.

Figure 2 *The Socio-Professional Situation*

LEVEL 1	LEVEL 2	LEVEL 3
EVENT TGIF (*Happy Hour*)	COMPONENTS • MANAGING INTERRUPTIONS What if you're talking with a prof? Who starts again? • GREETINGS How do you greet professors/advisors? What do you say to peers/colleagues? • PAYING / TIPPING / LEAVING Who and when do you tip? Who pays? How do you split/*divvy* up? How do you figure out a tip? Who do you leave the tip with if you leave before the others? How do you leave early? • REFUSING ALCOHOLIC DRINKS How do you say no? What can you say besides *no*? Do you have to order something? • FOLLOWING MULTIPLE CONVERSATIONS How do you listen when more than one person's talking? • ASKING FOR REPETITION/CLARIFICATION How many times can you ask? • ENCOUNTERING / REACTING TO HUMOR What do you do when you hear a dirty joke?	LANGUAGE FOCUS

Adapted by Imber/Parker from Ellis & Johnson.
Teaching Business English. Oxford, 1994

Having identified a situation and ferreted out some of its components, the focus narrows further. This point marks the transition to the third step, in which some specific language structures are selected for practice in building greater fluency control. Students and instructor together select a component to begin with, e.g., interruptions. The teacher then determines the specific language focus areas. For example, for handling interruptions one might focus on identifying and using appropriate speech acts (also called gambits or verbal stratagems) for interruptions and within that category, appropriate remarks and registers for returning, for instance, from an interruption by a peer as opposed to an interruption by a superior or professor. Another possibility would be to choose modals and colloquialisms, to help with such issues as knowing what to do if one does not drink alcoholic beverages.

When working with these situational components and language focus areas it soon becomes apparent that although specific speech acts and emphasis will differ in relation to student as well as to situational needs, many of the same language structures are used for all socio-professional events. Since the language focus is repetitive, it provides students excellent practice in learning to extrapolate from one event to another.

Having brought the students to this point, the teacher now faces the challenge of teaching:

a) the selected language focus areas
b) in the selected component(s)
c) of the selected situation.

There are several options in response to this challenge. One is to start from scratch and design a course or write a text in fluency for socio-professional discourse. Another is to examine what is already in place and re-design existing courses to put more emphasis on this register. A third, and to us far more expedient way, is to refocus techniques and materials already in use in existing classwork. Given the circumstances of most ESL teachers, this third option seems the most immediately viable, and is demonstrated through the following examples.

ACTIVITIES

There is no doubt that macro-techniques such as simulations and role plays are extremely valuable and we strongly recommend them. In addition, however, we have found micro techniques as basic as discrete point analysis to be equally valuable. Furthermore, micro-techniques tend to maximize learner involvement in self-monitoring. They can be effective even in courses such as pronunciation, where the focus is frequently perceived as too narrow to include activities in socio-professional discourse.

To demonstrate the effectiveness of this micro approach, we have chosen a sample activity from a pronunciation course. Determining Lexical Register (see Figure 3), is an activity from a pronunciation course. The chart is used to classify words and expressions by level of formality. In the worksheet shown, interruptions have been selected for study. Examples for each level are listed in the middle column. The left column is used to enter more expressions, again, elicited as far as possible from students themselves. Discussion can then center on which level each term belongs to, or the students can be asked to first apply them and then look at the question of appropriate level.

In the latter case, students write a brief dialogue or conversation, in this case involving a professor, a student, and a waiter at a TGIF. They use some of the interruption terms just discussed may even choose to expand the script somewhat. For instance, here they have been asked to include modals.

Figure 4 contains an example of a script written by students.

Now the teacher can guide the class in making corrections. In the sample shown, discussion can focus on the interruption expressions, the level of formality of the modals used, and whether those modals are appropriate in meaning and register to the speakers and the situations. In addition, intonation, word stress, and linking can be practiced.

Figure 3 *Determining Lexical Register: Social Contexts of Vocabulary **

The following chart indicates levels of formality of lexical items, ranging from 5 (most formal) to 1 (least formal). As you work with your terms/phrases you will find a fair amount of overlap, especially among levels 2, 3 and 4.

VERBAL STRATAGEMS	LEVEL & DESCRIPTION	CONVERSATION
MANAGING INTERRUPTIONS *Sorry.* *Shut up!* *Do you mind!* *Where was I?* *As I was saying...* *Excuse me.*	**5** EF = Extremely Formal Used mainly in interactions requiring a very high degree of politeness. *E.g.* **If you would be so kind as to permit me to continue.**	
	4 GF = Generally Formal Used in interactions requiring some politeness. *E.g.* **To continue...**	
	3 CU = Commonly Used Used in a wide range of interactions; ranges from friendly conversations to media language; always appropriate. *E.g.* **As I was saying...**	
	2 IF = Informal Used in casual everyday speech; includes colloquial expressions, regional vocabulary and slang. *E.g.* **Where was I?**	
	1 LA = Limited Appropriateness Used mainly in special circumstances; often unacceptable for public interactions; includes profanity and intimate terms. *E.g.* **Shut up and lemme finish!**	

* *Adapted by Imber/Parker from Marshall Murray, Brigham Young University, 1993*

Figure 4 *Example of script written by students*

<table>
<tr><th>VERBAL STRATAGEMS</th><th>LEVEL & DESCRIPTION</th><th>CONVERSATION</th></tr>
<tr><td rowspan="5">MANAGING INTERRUPTIONS
Sorry.
Shut up!
Do you mind!
Where was I?
As I was saying...
Excuse me.</td><td>**5** EF = Extremely Formal

Used mainly in interactions requiring a very high degree of politeness.

E.g. **If you would be so kind as to permit me to continue.**</td><td rowspan="5">**Roles**: Professor (P)
Student (S)
Waitress (W)

Event: TGIF at *Dooley's*

Conversation:

P Jun, I want to suggest you to make some changes in the computer code you're working on.

S Of course. You'd better tell me.

W Excuse me...Another round, anyone?

P Yes, for me, please.

S Me too, sir.

P OK, where was I?

S You suggest me to make changes...</td></tr>
<tr><td>**4** GF = Generally Formal

Used in interactions requiring some politeness.

E.g. **To continue...**</td></tr>
<tr><td>**3** CU = Commonly Used

Used in a wide range of interactions; ranges from friendly conversations to media language; always appropriate.

E.g. **As I was saying...**</td></tr>
<tr><td>**2** IF = Informal

Used in casual everyday speech; includes colloquial expressions, regional vocabulary and slang.

E.g. **Where was I?**</td></tr>
<tr><td>**1** LA = Limited Appropriateness

Used mainly in special circumstances; often unacceptable for public interactions; includes profanity and intimate terms.

E.g. **Shut up and lemme finish!**</td></tr>
</table>

* *Adapted by Imber/Parker from Marshall Murray, Brigham Young University, 1993*

After rehearsing their scripts, students can be taped (audio or video) and critiqued. A form listing possible categories for critiquing (see Figure 5) is suggested to focus student listening and prevent meaningless global comments. In a large class, one or two presentations can be selected per session, and a few students act as "selected critics"; alternatively, groups of students can critique selected areas. For instance, in the sample dialogue shown in Figure 4, one group can focus on appropriate register, particularly of the verbal stratagems, another on the questioner's intonation, one on use and register of modals, and one on the responder's intonation. It should be noted that it is not necessary, nor even desirable, to comment on each category. One finding per student critic is enough for meaningful feedback, and it is likely that findings will be distributed across categories.

Figure 5 *Critique form*

SPEAKER'S NAME: CRITIQUED BY

1. Verbal Stratagems Used
   -
   -
   -
   -

2. Lexical Register Level # _______?

   Appropriate? [] Yes [] Perhaps [] No

3. Intonation Rating

   As questioner 1.........2.........3.........4.........5 (*highest*)

   As responder 1.........2.........3.........4.........5 (*highest*)

4. Language Focus:

   - Modals
   -
   -

5. Additional Comments:

This seemingly simple critique technique has proven to be a very productive way to make students active participants in the learning process and to help them recognize that they can learn not only from the instructor, but also from other NNSs. This in turn means that students can continue their learning when they are not in the classroom and after the course ends. A further benefit is that it helps improve listening skills.

CONCLUSION

Based on our interviews, it appears that, in general, there is an implicit expectation that is not being met - the need for overt language instruction in the socio-professional discourse register in EAP/ESP courses. Furthermore, we have found that while socio-professional discourse is extremely complex, it is possible, via our multi-level needs approach, to create materials and activities that will help students navigate the role structures inherent in the socio-professional situations they encounter. Additionally, the focus-group approach micro-manages the discourse areas most relevant to students' needs, making it easier for teachers to create instructional materials and activities which, in turn, will make it easier for students to grasp some of the intricacies of socio-professional discourse.

REFERENCES

Huckin, T.N. and Olsen, L.A. (1991) *Technical Writing and Professional Communication for Nonnative Speakers of English.* 2nd Edition. New York: McGraw Hill.

Swales, J. (1993) "Language and Success: Lessons to and From the United States. *Language, Learning and Success: Studying Through English* . Ed. George M. Blue. London: Modern English Publications and the British Council. 14-24

The Student as Linguist: A Technique for Helping Students Produce Genre Specific Grammatical Descriptions

Richard Badger
University of Stirling

INTRODUCTION

In recent years I have been involved in courses for students who wish to take or are taking degrees in law in English. One of the difficulties of such courses is deciding what kind of tasks best help these students. One obvious source of help is linguistic analyses of the language of the law. This is a topic which has been investigated in some depth in recent years (see for example Bhatia (1993), Gibbons (1994), Riley (1991), Russell and Locke (1992)). This research provides useful guidance for the language teacher though I would note Howe's (1993) comment that much of it:

> *... should be read with caution. The text description may be misleading in that it is limited to the examination of only one script, or even part of one script: the methodology described may be quite unrelated to law.*

Most of this research could be described as the discourse analysis of legal texts. This approach has produced many useful insights into the way in which legal texts are structured and provides the EAP/ESP teacher with many ideas for classroom activities. However, my students also have difficulties with the grammar of English and it is more difficult for the teacher to see how the research helps with grammar.

One approach is to assume that the grammar of specialised texts is the same as the grammar of what we might call general English and to adopt the same approach to this component of the course as would be done in a course in English for General Purposes. This is a common approach but it has, at least, two drawbacks. Firstly, the extent to which the language of the law, or any other specific field, is the same as 'general English' is unclear. Secondly, students find it hard to see the relevance of general English to their future studies.

One possible solution would be for teachers to carry out research into whatever registers or genres of English are relevant to their students. Time and resources unfortunately mean that this is not a feasible solution for most English Language Teaching (ELT) practitioners.

An alternative is to adopt a student centred approach with the students carrying out their own research with some outside help. This has the advantage that it provides the students with strategies which they can use to carry out their own investigations of texts outside the classroom. This does not mean that students will be conscious that they are carrying out these investigations but that having practiced these skills the students will apply them automatically.

> *Strategies begin as declarative knowledge that can become proceduralized with practice ... If the strategy application has become proceduralized .. the students may not be aware of using the strategy (O'Malley and Chamot 1990)*

In what follows I will describe how I prepared my own students to carry out this research, focussing on the use of the definite article in legal texts. However, it may be useful if I first describe my students.

THE STUDENTS

The students were doing a one year access or foundation course. At the end of the year they would hope to be accepted to start undergraduate Law or Business degrees. During the foundation year they took courses in English but also had content classes in Law, Business Studies and Communications. The students came from a range of linguistic backgrounds and generally had an upper intermediate or advanced level of English.

THE TECHNIQUE

The technique has three stages:

1. Choosing an area of grammar
2. Using the text for communication
3. Analysing the text.

1. Choosing an area of grammar

The first stage of the preparation was to decide which area of grammar needed to be examined. My needs analysis was largely based on errors in the students' writing, plus those grammatical areas that the students said they found difficult. It is important, for reasons of motivation, that the students understand that the grammatical areas are based on their specific problems and do not derive from some arbitrary list in a text book. The topics I have considered include the use of some prepositions, qualification in nominal groups, tense and aspect, conjunctions and, what I will be looking at here, the definite article.

If we accept that there are differences in grammar between different registers or genres, it is important that the materials which are used to exemplify particular grammatical areas are drawn from genres which relate to the students' areas of study. The texts used here were law reports. These are printed regularly in broadsheet newspapers in the UK. They have the advantage of being authentic legal documents and of being relatively easily accessible to teachers but there is no reason why extracts from official law reports, statutes or text books should not be used. A full list of the law reports is given at the end of this paper.

Having chosen an area of grammar, the next sub-stage was to provide the students with a description of the definite article. The following is a selection from some standard grammars:

The word 'the' is a specific determinative Deictic of a peculiar kind: it means 'the subset in question is identifiable; but this will not tell you how to identify it - the information is somewhere around, where you can recover it. ' (Halliday 1985)

The definite article the is used to mark the phrase it introduces as definite ie as 'referring to something which can be identified uniquely in the contextual or general knowledge shared by speaker and hearer'. (Quirk et al. 1985)

You can use a noun group consisting of just 'the' and a noun when you are referring to a specific person or thing, to a specific group of people or things and you know that the person you are talking or writing to will understand which person thing or group you are referring to. (Sinclair 1990)

These sorts of explanations are difficult to criticise and I am sure most teachers have made use of something rather like them on several occasions. However, they are expressed in very general terms and it is often hard for students and teachers to see how they can be applied to particular stretches of English.

So I then turned to a more delicate description offered by Berry (1993). This description makes use of the following set of categories:

1. referring:	But then I came on a man playing a harp. It was a black harp ... and the man was dressed as a gorilla.
2. synonyms:	There was an enormous cat crouching on the counter. The animal looked up at Mrs Bixby.
3. associated:	You live in Paris. The address is in your passport.
4. qualified nouns:	The price of copper
5. superlative adjectives:	This isn't the best camping country.
6. unique adjectives:	They even use the same lawyers.
7. generic:	The Russians are no less perceptive.
8. situational:	(At a meal) Pass the salt.

(Adapted from Berry 1993)

Berry's descriptions are relatively easy to understand. For example his statement about associative uses of the definite article could easily be applied by students:

If you want to talk about something that is associated with an earlier item (even though you haven't mentioned it before) you can use the definite article to show that there is a relationship or association between the items.

So when presented with

When the victim of a criminal attack dies after medical treatment during which the doctors failed to diagnose a rare complication, the jury in the murder trial of the attacker must assess whether the attacker's acts contributed significantly to the victim's death. (Regina v Cheshire) most students can offer an explanation of 'the' in 'the attacker' on the basis of the link with 'a criminal attack'.

Similarly, students find it easy to understand why the superlative adjective in nominal groups such as 'the most difficult cases' (Aldridge v BT) requires a definite article.

However, the last two of Berry's categories, generic and situational uses of the definite article, were harder to apply. For example, is 'the immigration laws' in the following extract generic?

> *Lord Justice Glidewell said that section 33 (1) of the Immigration Act 1971 defined "illegal entrant" as a person unlawfully entering or seeking to enter in breach of a deportation order or of the immigration laws, and also includes a person who has so entered. (Regina v Home Secretary, ex parte Adesina)*

Again the term situational assumes that you know which aspect of the world is relevant to the text and only expert readers of specialist texts have this information.

The students were provided with copies of Berry's categories and the definitions mentioned above and we discussed them in general terms. Their attention was drawn to the fact that there were some difficulties with the categories and also that there was no guarantee that the categories would cover all uses of the definite article in law reports.

2. Using the text for communication

There is always a danger that grammatical analysis will be treated as an end in itself rather than a means to communicate. One way to avoid this danger is for the students to use texts in a manner that approximates as closely as possible to ways in which they would be used in the target situation before using the texts as examples of a particular linguistic feature. Within the framework of genre analysis this means using the texts for a purpose that mirrors as closely as possible the purpose for which they would be used in 'real' life.

As noted above, the texts used were law reports printed in broadsheet newspapers. Lawyers use law reports as a source of principles of law rather in the way Aesop's fables are the source of moral principles. Discovering the legal principle underlying a law report is a very specialised skill. Fortunately most law reports start with a summary of the report and often this summary includes the principle of law which can be derived from the report.

The students were provided with a version of the law report I had chosen to look at in that class. This version did not include the summary section. With the help of dictionaries and any other aid they required they produced summaries and identified the relevant legal principle. They then compared their summary with the official summary and discussed any differences.

3. Analysing the text

Having treated the text as a part of a communicative task the students now treat the law report as a linguistic artefact. There are two versions of this stage as applied to the definite article, but in both the students were given complete copies of the law report. Initially the students were asked to identify examples of Berry's categories. One advantage of this is that the teacher can carry out the exercise beforehand and so predict more or less what the students will do with the text. My students enjoyed this and seemed to learn something, if only the meta-language connected with the definite article. However, limiting the students to the Berry categories implied that the categories were not open to criticism and the existence of a kind of model answer encouraged students to play the game of guessing what the teacher wants rather than investigating what might be useful to themselves.

The second, and more useful version, is one I describe as the blind leading the blind, because it is very difficult for teachers using this technique to predict what the students will produce. As before the students were provided with complete versions of the law report. However this time some definite nominal groups were highlighted. These were selected on the basis of the following criteria: the head had not appeared earlier in the text (this was to exclude most examples of referring definite articles); and there was no modification or qualification (which was intended to exclude qualified nouns, and superlative and unique adjectives). The criteria I used were what testing experts call 'quick and dirty', and could be easily carried out using the search function on any word processor.

The students then produced a classification of uses of the definite articles in the particular text. As far as possible these classifications covered all the highlighted definite articles in the law report and avoided catch-all categories such as 'miscellaneous'. As one would expect, different labels for categories were produced by different groups of students though there was a large amount of agreement about what went in each category, and also a considerable degree of overlap with Berry's categories.

However, the students produced two categories which struck me as interesting. The first was a category of legal terms, such as 'plaintiff', 'decision', 'facts', and 'legislation'. This covered a range of words which were closely related to law case and law reports. The second was what is variously called phrases or idioms and included items such as 'in the round', and 'to reverse the coin'.

Once the students had agreed a set of categories, one of them produced a typed version of the list which was given to all students in the class in the hope that they would use it to deal with any problems they had with the definite article.

EVALUATION

This technique offers a way of dealing with some of the problems associated with ESP. The main advantages of the technique are firstly it allows a non-specialist to deal with a specialist text without getting involved in debates of the role of the English and the Law teacher. Secondly, it provides motivation for students to look at grammar. While there is no statistical evidence for this claim, it seems to me that this technique has made the students more aware of a range of grammatical areas and improved students' accuracy in writing. Thirdly, it allows the language teacher to look at specialist texts for which we have incomplete linguistic descriptions. Also it gives the teacher an insight into how learners see grammatical aspects of English, and learners' views do not always coincide with those of teachers or linguists. Fourthly, it encourages student independence. In terms of their specialist area the technique shows students that they are able to understand difficult texts on their own. In terms of language learning, students can use the technique on any text they wish and, hopefully, come to realise that they can generate their own grammatical description of the language where current grammars are incomplete. The students become more aware of the link between grammatical choice and meaning, and thus become more efficient and independent language learners.

REFERENCES

Alderson, J. C. and Urquhart, A. H. (eds.). (1984) *Reading in a Foreign Language* London: Longman.

Berry, R. (1993) *Collins COBUILD English Guides 3: Articles* London: HarperCollins

Bhatia, V. K. (1993) *Analysing Genre: Language in Professional Settings* London: Longman.

Gibbons, J. (ed.) (1994) *Language and the Law* Harlow: Longman.

Halliday, M. A. K. (1985) *An introduction to functional grammar* London: Edward Arnold.

Howe, P. (1993) 'Planning a Pre-Sessional Course in English for Academic Legal Purposes' in G. M. Blue (ed. Language, Learning and Success: Studying through English London: Macmillan.

Levi, J. N. and Graffam Waler, A. (1990) *Language in the Judicial Process* New York: Plenum Press.

O'Malley, J, and Chamot A. (1990) *Learning Strategies in Second Language Acquisition* Cambridge: CUP.

Quirk, R. , Greenbaum, S., Leech, G., and Svartvik, J. (1985) *A Comprehensive Grammar of the English Language* Harlow: Longman.

Riley, A. (1991) *English for Law* London: Macmillan.

Russell, F. and Locke, C. (1992) *English Law and Language: An introduction for students of English* London: Cassell.

Sinclair, J. (1990) Collins Cobuild English Grammar London: Glasgow.

The Texts

1. Aldridge v British Telecommunications plc The Times 6 October 1989
2. Regina v Home Secretary, ex parte Adesina The Guardian February 18 1988
3. Al-Kandari v J. R. Brown & Co The Guardian 1 March 1988
4. Benham v Poole Borough Council The Guardian 23 October 1991
5. Regina v Cheshire The Guardian 30 April 1991
6. Cleveland Museum of Art v Capricorn International SA & Another The Times 4 October 1989.

Research Articles in Science: A Comparative Study of Linguistic Choices

Ann Montemayor-Borsinger
University of Glasgow and Instituto Balseiro (UNC - CNEA)

INTRODUCTION

In recent years a growing number of studies have focused on academic writing, and in particular on the generic characteristics of scientific writing. This study focuses more specifically on the choices authors can make when writing up what seems to be a very restricted genre. In particular it investigates the extent to which certain linguistic variables affect the way different authors organise and present similar experiments in distinct ways.

To capture this system of choice a comparative analysis is made of two texts taken from a restricted sub-genre, that of the article in Non-Newtonian Fluid Mechanics, in an attempt to show how discourse is a system of choice not only across genres but also within genres (Swales 1990). One paper is Canadian in origin, the other was published by MIT (Mass. Inst. of Tech).

This work does not focus on whether a text is successful or not in 'absolute terms' since the texts have been published in first rate journals within the field of research considered, and have been written by recognised scientists. Instead it attempts to investigate the extent to which Theme, understood as the first part of a clause, affects the way different authors organise and present relatively similar experiments in distinct ways. The analysis is based on Theme choice because in scientific Research Articles (RA) it appears that '*as part of a writer's available linguistic resources, the choice of first position in the sentence is significant*' (Gosden 1993). Gosden's observation, which agrees with the findings of authors such as Fries (1983), Martin (1985), Davies (1988) and Berry (1989), can be related to the Moves identified by Swales (1990) who shows that

> *...the foregrounding or thematizing of certain types of information according to the genre is one means through which writers can achieve both local discourse goals, for example, the signalling of 'Moves' within one RA section and, more globally, the interplay of interactional and topic-based Themes throughout RA discourse.*

The texts were selected on the basis of interviews with scientists who commented upon the significant differences they had noticed in the organisation of the Numerical Results section of two papers in Non-Newtonian Fluid Mechanics. The scientists were interested to know whether there were any linguistic aspects of the two texts that could help understand the way they were organised. They were especially interested in the fact that, although both papers were extremely 'readable', one was tailored to discuss unsuccessful but important results for the development of science, whereas the other paper was shorter, more conventionally patterned, and presented only successful results. A consideration for these concerns has led to the analysis of the texts.

The following section presents the method to be used in the analysis of the two texts. Section three discusses some of the findings and Section four suggests directions for pedagogical applications and future research.

METHOD OF ANALYSIS

Definition of theme

Fries (1983) notes that the consideration of what is or is not thematic within a given sentence varies. As defined by Halliday (1985), Theme is '*the element which serves as the point of departure of the message*'. Halliday also considers multiple Themes which can have simultaneously textual, interpersonal and ideational elements. The textual and interpersonal elements are optional, but '*There is always an ideational element in the Theme*' (Halliday 1985, bold as in the original text). One of the difficulties with Halliday's classification is that while defining ideational as '*the representation of experience*' and as '*meaning in the sense of 'content*'', he is not consistent in what he considers as containing an ideational component. This is especially significant for circumstantial adjuncts, as noticed by Davies (1997).

The analysis of the present study will include, following Davies (1988,1997), the grammatical subject as an obligatory element in Theme. In a similar way Berry (1989) includes in Theme '*everything that anyone working in the Hallidayan tradition has ever ... advocated including*' and treats as Theme '*everything that precedes the verb of the main clause*'. These extensions to Halliday's Theme give it more pedagogic potential: it is closer to what we feel Theme should be, perhaps because '*Subject is equated with the intuitive notion of 'what the clause is about*'' (Davies 1988). Davies thus postulates two, rather than one potential functions for Theme. These are '*identification of [obligatory] Topic, realised by Subject, and provision of [optional] Contextual Frame, realised by elements preceding Subject*' (Davies 1997, italics in original).

From now on this study will use the label of 'Subject/Topic' rather than just 'Topic', to make it absolutely clear that in the following analysis Topic is realised by subject. In addition the study analyses Theme only in main clauses to give a clearer picture of significant thematic patterns without the interference of secondary organisation.

Taxonomy of theme components used in this study

When the Subject/Topic of a sentence is conflated with Theme it is treated as unmarked. Gosden (1993) has discussed extensively what he calls Grammatical Subject, which functions as unmarked Theme '*unless a writer has a good reason for choosing something else*'. As Grammatical Subject functions as topical element, it is a recurrent element in discourse. This '*repeated occurrence ... of the same topical element ... as Subject is seen not only to specify Topic, but also to be the primary means by which the continuity of coherent discourse is achieved.*' (Davies, 1988).

When not only the Subject/Topic of a sentence is foregrounded, Theme is marked by a Contextual Frame whose function is to help '*the development of Topic as the discourse proceeds . . .*' (Davies 1997). To illustrate unmarked and marked Theme, Figure 1 and 2 are reproduced from Gosden (1993), with examples from the present corpus; Figure 2 shows in particular how the optional element of Contextual Frame marks Theme. The taxonomies used for the Discourse Functions of Topic and Contextual Frame are presented in the following section.

	The mesh M5	*is shown in Figure 3*
Grammatical Function:	GRAMMATICAL SUBJECT	
Discourse Function:	REAL-WORLD ENTITY	
Theme Component:	TOPIC	
Thematic Structure:	THEME	RHEME

Figure 1. Example of unmarked Theme (Gosden 1993)

	In the present case	*we*	*define De - Arw as ...*
Grammatical function:	ADJUNCT	SUBJECT	
Discourse Function:	LOCATION IN DISCOURSE	DISCOURSE PARTICIPANT	
Theme Component:	CONTEXT FRAME	TOPIC	
Thematic Structure:	THEME		RHEME

Figure 2. Example of marked Theme (Gosden 1993)

Discourse functions of topic

Because of Gosden's(1993) extensive work on unmarked Theme - conflated with obligatory Grammatical Subject and Topic - within the context of scientific writing, his taxonomy based on four domains has been adopted. The ordering of the four domains with their corresponding subdomains (examples in italics from the present corpus) is presented here from top to bottom and reflects the continuum from 'personally visible' to 'invisible' initially distinguished by Davies (1988) and developed by Gosden as a continuum from "the Participant to the Real World domain. Towards one end, it is typified by the increasingly overt presence of the writer as a visible participant in the research/reporting process; towards the other, there is a greater focus on research-based, i.e. real-world physical and mental entities and activities."

In the following explanation, the words in italics represent examples taken from the two papers analysed.

A. The **Participant domain** subdivided in Discourse Participant (*We...*), Participant Viewpoint (*Our tests...*) and Interactive Participant (*Keunings [19]...*)

B. The **Discourse domain** subdivided in Discourse Event/Process (*This point...*) and Micro Discourse Entity (*Figure 4...*).

C. The **Hypothesised and Objectivized domain**. The relevant subdomain for this study is Hypothesised entity, which consists of abstract concepts such as *theories, hypotheses* and *models.* Researchers often choose to put these entities in subject position, thus reducing author visibility. Furthermore, Davies (1988) emphasises that although the expert specialist immediately perceives the hypothetical nature of such entities, the novice might not because they appear in the text, '*together with evaluative comment, as objects with a greater than hypothetical status*'. This domain thus represents '*a wealth of subtle means by which writer's comments on hypotheses and viewpoints can be realised*' (Gosden 1993) and '*may be seen to represent the most discretely interactional Theme*' (ibid.).

D. The **Real-World domain**, subdivided into Mental Process (*Calculations with the smooth contraction...*); Real World entity (*The mesh M5...*) and Real World process/event (*Increasing the resolution of the mesh near this point...)*

Discourse functions of contextual frame

Davies (1997) has worked in detail on marked Theme and Contextual Frame. In her words, '*Unlike topical elements which are the recurring elements of coherent discourse, these framing elements are typically non-recurrent and as such signal changes/shifts or stages in the progression of the discourse*'. She adopts a semantic, rather than a grammatical categorisation because

> '*it allows for the inclusion, as examples of marked, and (multiple) theme, of elements which are not identified as such by Halliday, that is, the class of 'minimal' adjuncts represented by conjunctive and modal adjuncts and conjunctions and, in addition,* **a small set of thematic Subjects which are seen to be marked in their semantic role** *in that they do not identify participants, ..., but instead, appear to 'frame' the message by specifying discourse goals or projecting evaluation.*' (bold as in the original text)

Davies defines four categories of Discourse Functions for Contextual Frame:

A. **Location**. In the analysis that follows we only have **Location** in Discourse (*Here...*) and **Location** in Discourse Data (*For the finest mesh M5...*).

B. **Logical Relations/Progression**, embodied by linking adjuncts (comparison, addition, contrast, reason, consequence, condition, concession, apposition/restriction).

C. **Goal and Process**, a category that plays an ancillary role in this analysis.

D. **Evaluation**. As will be seen in the following section, the MIT paper has very few of these items, a typical example being *It seems clear that ...* whereas the Canadian paper has many more.

FINDINGS

General comments on the numerical results section of the two papers

This section analyses the entire Numerical Results section of the two articles which were selected on the basis of interviews with three scientists, two experienced researchers working in the field of Non-Newtonian Fluid Mechanics (NNFM) and the editor of the main journal in that field, the Journal of NNFM, where one of the papers was published. The main criterion for selection was comparability. One paper was written by a research team working at the Massachusetts Institute of Technology, and will be referred to as the MIT paper, and the other by a research team working in Canada, and will be referred to as the Canadian paper (see bibliography).

The Results Section of the MIT paper has over 2400 words, one table and 17 extremely complex figures which actually contain 39 separate figures within them. The Canadian paper has just under 900 words and five figures which subdivide into eleven. At a first glance we can see differences between the two papers, the MIT Numerical Results section being nearly three times longer and with nearly four times more figures than the Canadian one. For lack of space only a small excerpt from each text is reproduced in the following boxes.

MIT TEXT: Brown et al - Theme in bold characters

A limiting value of De = De,, was computed in the family of solutions to (3.4) that evolved continuously from De = 0 for all five finite element meshes, **and its value** is plotted in Fig. 5 as a function of the total number of unknowns. **The value of DeL** was very sensitive to mesh refinement, especially in the region near the corner. **Increasing the resolution of the mesh near this point** decreased DeL. **For the finest mesh M5 steady solutions** were found only for De *<DeL= 0.1. **Keunings [19]** has seen a similar decrease in the maximum obtainable De for calculations with the Ucm fluid in the same geometry with even more extensive regular mesh refinement. **The centerline velocity profile and the axial velocity field across the contraction plane** are shown in Fig. 6 for De=0.1. **Both profiles** are free of oscillations. **The stress field** has oscillations in the region near the corner, as is seen from the axial normal stress plotted along the wall of the small tube in Fig. 7. **The additional refinement supplied by mesh M5 over M4** increases both the spatial frequency and the amplitude of the oscillations in the region. **The value De=0.1** corresponds to the limiting De for the mesh M5, but not for mesh M4.

CANADIAN TEXT: Fortin et al - Themes in bold characters

We tested three different meshes (Fig. 5). **Mesh A** is a relatively coarse, almost uniform grid **while mesh B** is a refinement (by a factor of 2) of the former. **Mesh C** is non-uniform and has been refined near the singularity. **Let us first consider what happens when the Deborah number** increases on mesh C. **For De = 0.8 (Fig. 6a) a section of T*1 through the singularity (on the line y = 3 of Fig. 4)** shows a sharp peak, not very different, although higher from what is observed in the Newtonian case. **For *De*= 1.6, the peak** has grown **and small oscillations** begin to appear (Fig. 6b). **Finally, at *De*= 2.0, the result** is unacceptable (Fig. 6c). **Appearance of oscillations** is linked with a spurious change of type ... **This is a clear indication that the upwinding technique** is not strong enough. **This should not be a surprise since a second order scheme** cannot be TDV for a transport equation of the type we have for

Comparative analysis of topic

Table 1 shows that the MIT text is far more impersonal and less interactional than the Canadian one: although about 40% of the Topics are in the Hypothesised and Objectivized Domain - which we have seen is a *discretely* interactional domain - more than half of them are in the Real World Domain, where the author is entirely invisible. The Canadian text has nearly 60% of its Topics in the Hypothesised and Objectivized Domain, followed by the high writer-visibility Participant Domain, with the Real World Domain only in third position. This implies that 80% of the Topics of the Canadian paper possess an interactional character, whereas in the MIT paper less than half of the Topics have an interactional character, and not a very strong one at that.

Table 1 Distribution of Topic

Topics	*MIT*		*CANADIAN*	
Total	107		52	
Participant Domain	6	(6%)	12	(23%)
Discourse Domain	1	(1%)	1	(2%)
Hypothesised&Objectivized Domain	44	(41%)	29	(56%)
Real World Domain	56	(52%)	10	(19%)

Comparative analysis of contextual frame

The MIT paper has only 24 Themes marked by Contextual Frame (CF) out of a total of 107 Themes. The Canadian paper has 35 marked Themes out of 55, five of the CFs clearly combining two of the CF classes distinguished by Davies(1997), making them longer and more complicated than in MIT. As for Topic, CFs in the Canadian text are more interactive, with nearly half of them presenting Evaluation. In both the MIT and the Canadian texts one third of the CFs has to do with Logical Relations. But as the MIT text is three times longer than the Canadian one, this means MIT has a far lower density of connectives. Finally, nearly half of the CFs in MIT are in Location, and more precisely Location in Discourse Data, thus reinforcing the high topicality of this text.

Table 2 Distribution of Contextual Frame

Contextual Frame	*MIT*		*CANADIAN*	
Total	24		40	(5 double)
Location	11	(46%)	7	(18%)
Logical Relations	8	(33%)	13	(33%)
Goal and Process	2	(8%)	2	(5%)
Evaluation	3	(13%)	18	(45%)

Added insights on theme

a) Theme density in the texts

Table 3 shows the number of words in the whole text, in Theme, in Contextual Frame and in Topic. On the basis of these numbers, the relative weight of Theme and its components is determined. More than 40% of the words in the Canadian text are in Theme compared to 30% for MIT, the greatest difference lying in the relative weight of Contextual Frame: 23% of the words in the Canadian text are in CFs - nearly half of which evaluate - compared to only 7% for MIT; in Topic the distribution is more similar, although as expected MIT has a higher percentage than the Canadian paper.

Table 3 Theme density in the two texts

	MIT	*CANADIAN*
Total words in text	2433	899
Words in Theme	724	374
Words in Contextual Frame	160	207
Words in Topic	564	167
Words in Theme/Total words in text	30%	42%
Words in Context. Frame/Total words in text	7%	23%
Words in Topic/Total words in text	23%	19%

b) Lexical density of theme

Following Martin (1985) in his analysis of the differences between two factual texts, a brief study of the lexical density in the Theme of the two papers is shown in table 4. Here the most significant feature is a higher overall lexical density for Theme in MIT, especially in Topic. Compared with the Canadian text, there is practically no CF in MIT, and far more lexical information is packed in the Topic slot. The Canadian paper is more people orientated - with long, interactive Contexts. There are many more link words, perhaps to force sentence organisation. The impression given is that the underlying structure of MIT organises through a succession of lexically dense and precise Topics, whereas in the Canadian paper link words are needed to do that.

Table 4 Lexical density in Theme

	MIT	*CANADIAN*
Words in Theme	724	374
Lexical words in Theme	423	174
Lexical words in Contextual Frame	63	83
Lexical words in Topic	360	91
Lexical density in Theme	58%	47%
Lexical density in Context. Frame	39%	40%
Lexical density in Topic	64%	54%

CONCLUSIONS

The current study has shown that even within the highly restricted genre of the research article in Non-Newtonian Fluid Mechanics there are important language choices to be made. This reinforces the findings of studies such as Bazerman (1984) who not only agrees with the traditional view that science is a rational, cumulative, corporate enterprise, but also points out that '*this enterprise is realised only through linguistic, rhetorical and social means and* ***choices****, all with epistemological consequences*' (emphasis added). Bazerman further considers that studies of scientific texts should consider the linguistic tools available to scientists, and the implications of those tools: '*Even as the conventions constrain a writer, they [the tools] may be mobilised and manipulated to the writer's advantage. In whatever form the conventions make their presence felt, they are the basis of many writing choices.*' (ibid., brackets added)

In the cases considered here, the MIT text deals with complexity by topicalising, with very little evaluation. It has no qualms about presenting failures, although it does subtly comment and hypothesise in Topic. The Canadian text, seen as conforming more to a stereotyped view of science where only successful results are presented, requires evaluation. It speaks more to the reader, and wants to win him over, to convince him that what has been done is sound.

In more general terms the study has made explicit the use of Theme in the discussion of results and has shown how information can be packed in the Subject/Topic slot thus helping the discussion of detailed results by making a text flow with relatively simple Themes, as illustrated in the MIT text. The study has also shown that a different option is to make the text more interactive by a heavier use of Contextual Frames, which specify discourse goals and/or project evaluation, as illustrated in the Canadian text. Knowledge of these options and of the way insiders perceive these options should not only facilitate the analysis of scientific texts, but also provide a basis for pedagogical applications.

With this in mind novice researchers could be encouraged to opt in a first instance for certain patterns for the presentation of successful results, building up, as they publish successive research articles, a Results Section more tailored to their outlook on science and the way they work. Whatever the pattern adopted, it should be taken for what it is: not as an immutable blueprint that ought to be followed forever, but as an illustration of how results can be presented and as a basis upon which more personal ways of writing can be explored.

REFERENCES

Berry M. (1989) Thematic Options and Success in Writing *Language & Literature - Theory and Practice,* University of Nottingham.

Bazerman C. (1984) Modern Evolution of the Experimental Report in Physics: Spectroscopic Articles in *Physical Review,* 1893-1980 in *Social Studies of Science* Vol 14, 163-196.

Brown R.A., Armstrong R.C., Beris A.N. and Yeh P.-W. (1986) Galerkin finite element analysis of complex viscoelastic flows *Computer Methods in Applied Mechanics,* 58, 201-226.

Davies F. (1988) "Reading between the lines: Thematic choice as a device for presenting written viewpoint in academic discourse" *ESPecialist,* Vol. 9, Nos 1/2, 173-200.

Davies F. (1997) "Marked Theme as a Heuristic for Analysing Text-Type, Text and Genre" In Pique J. And Viera D.J. (Eds) *Applied Linguistics: Theory and Practice in ESP* Valencia University Press.

Fortin M. and Fortin A. (1989) A new approach for the FEM simulation of viscoelastic flows *Journal of Non-Newtonian Fluid Mechanics,* 32, 295-310

Fries P. (1983) On the Status of Theme in English: Arguments for Discourse" in Pertofi J.S. and Sozer E. *Micro and Macro Connexity of Texts* Papers in Text Linguistics Helmut Burk

Gosden H. (1993) "Discourse Functions of Subject in Scientific Research Articles" in *Applied Linguistics,* Vol. 14, No 1, Oxford University Press

Halliday M.A.K. (1985) *An Introduction to Functional Grammar* Edward Arnold Publisher
Martin J.R. (1985) *Factual writing: exploring and challenging social reality* Oxford University Press
Swales, J. (1990) *Genre Analysis: English in Academic and Research Settings* Cambridge University Press

PART THREE:

EAP AND CLASSROOM PERSPECTIVES

Hidden Agendas and the Pursuit of Linguistic Excellence

Katie Gray
Oxford University

Current methodologies emphasize the importance of learner centred teaching and of developing learner autonomy. The research literature abounds in analyses of differences in motivation, in learning strategies and in learning styles. Teachers have no problem in recognising individual differences in their students; the problem is developing a practical way of dealing with these differences. This paper takes a pragmatic look at the relevant research in order to pull out ideas for classroom practice and then examines their application in the context of an in-sessional class.

THE PARADOX

Do we pay sufficient attention to what students want from a course? Do students want the linguistic excellence we assume for them? We often take it for granted that they want to sustain a steady improvement in language, and measure progress accordingly: we divide them into ability groups, we categorize them informally in staffroom discussions according to an implied scale, we write reports on this basis. Beyond what we see, their different performances as product, we fail to pay attention to other process differences. Yet we know the importance of differing learning styles, of individual differences in motivation and aptitude. The literature abounds with many details of the variables which influence language, so we are not unaware of well-recognised factors - such as attitude towards the language and the language classroom, concern for grades, risk-taking, sociability - which mean that within the classroom context the path to proficiency is in no sense direct.

We know too that our own attitudes to the teaching/learning process constitute another set of particularly important variables. Even though we may well include cultural awareness activities in our lessons, we cannot avoid imposing on our students our own linguistic and cultural values - for example our model of the good student and of the good language learner. The idea of negotiated syllabuses is not new, but how many of us use our insights into the differences between our learners to discover what their beliefs about the nature of language learning are, and what precise motivation they bring with them, *in order to accommodate these into our teaching?* As busy classroom teachers confronted with a pre-sessional class made up of students of different nationalities, different ages and experience, and with different types of sponsors, we might recognize the need for differentiation and understanding, but we do not normally have the time to take all this into account. One way out of this paradoxical situation is to use action research. By following up practical conclusions arrived at by the theoreticians, and incorporating them into our teaching, we might be in a position to understand and to motivate our students in a variety of new ways.

A PRACTICAL READING OF THE THEORY

Putting the learner centre stage

Skehan (1989) reviews the major research into individual differences. While useful, and clearly written, his book is somewhat disappointing. The author emphasizes the immense difficulty of coming up with theoretically based descriptions of individual differences, let alone with an account of how some of the posited variables might interact with one another. Yet in his final chapter he offers some intriguing conclusions. He neatly pinpoints how, despite bringing the learner to centre stage, both the ESP movement and the concern for individualization of instruction have *rather curiously, side-stepped the actual learner* (ibid.). ESP is accused of focusing too much on students' needs and not paying sufficient attention to how terminal competence is to be achieved, while the individualization movement has addressed this issue by providing large quantities of attractive and stimulating materials but has failed to link the provision of choice to learner characteristics. Here are two useful suggestions to be followed up in the pre-sessional class.

Differing motivations

Any analysis of individual differences has to acknowledge the importance of motivation. Skehan goes beyond Gardner and Lambert's well-known distinction between instrumental and integrative motivation by drawing attention to their later model

motivation = effort + desire to achieve a goal + attitude

which provides another useful insight into how internal and external pressures interact to produce motivation. 'Effort' is here seen as instrumentally driven by a desire to please the teacher, by good study habits and by pressure of exams, though not necessarily in a language specific way. On the other hand the 'desire to achieve a goal' is both language specific and integrative, and 'attitudes' are perceived as a sustaining base affecting behaviour and produced by social milieu. The importance accorded here to attitude variables in motivation again points to positive ways in which learners might be encouraged to change.

Differing strategies

Teachers want to develop successful learners and know that they have to effect change in their students' attitudes, but feel most confident dealing closer to the surface with learning strategies where control over the learning process seems more immediately achievable. Skehan surveys the research on these and underlines the number of different ways of categorising strategies. He points out that the most useful classification is O'Malley et al's (1985), which distinguishes between metacognitive, cognitive and social strategies. Richards and Lochart (1994) also support these findings almost ten years later.

However before embarking on the development of such strategies in the classroom it is worth noting the tentative suggestion from Horwitz (1987) that *erroneous beliefs about language may lead to less effective language learning strategies* and that *beliefs about language learning may be more susceptible to teacher intervention* - than cognitive style and affective variables. In other words it may be best to start the process of developing effective strategies by opening a discussion on beliefs on language learning.

Differing study competences

It may be more practical to think of discussing learning strategies and beliefs about language learning than to think about changing attitudes. In fact though, most EAP courses focus on the development of study skills as the most achievable way of positively affecting the learning process. Waters and Waters (1992) help point to the flaw in such an approach. They look at the teaching of study skills - that is to say at techniques for effective study rather than learning strategies. They make the point that, until study competence is in place, study skills are only superficial techniques that cannot be used effectively by the learner. To define study competence they invoke the cognitive and affective characteristics of the successful student, such as self-awareness, logical thinking, critical questioning, independence of mind, and self-confidence (ibid.). With such a student there would be no tension between personal agenda and a desire for linguistic excellence. Clearly if we could, by using the awareness and discovery techniques Waters and Waters suggest, encourage each of our students to develop into mature individuals, with open, questioning minds, with an active independent approach to study there would be no problem of either motivation or of linguistic success. Of course we are being asked to deepen the way we do skills training and it seems we cannot avoid dealing with cognitive affective variables, even if we keep in mind Horwitz' warning about the difficulty of just such a change.

Changing classroom practice

Here then are a number of ideas to be tried out in the classroom, although each one may possibly cause as many problems as it solves. As language teachers our professionalism orientates us towards developing 'good students' and 'good language learners'. Yet because students are different, with different wants, different characteristics, different attitudes, different motivations, we are bound to fail with some of them. We have to learn that respecting individual differences entails respecting those who are not, and who do not want to be, good language learners. Even then the flexible approach that would seem to be indicated by a survey of the research will create difficulties, since such an approach may well conflict with the idea that many students have of the teacher's role. Students are often not prepared for teachers to be reflective, considerate of their wants, and eager to negotiate. In order to break this potentially vicious circle, changes of classroom management, of methods, materials and assessment criteria have to be only very gradually introduced, openly discussed with the students, and constantly fine-tuned as their effect is observed.

This is what I attempted in a year long piece of action research. The specific context for putting theory into practice was a monolingual insesssional class, made up of Taiwanese civil servants. Ironically in such a class it is easier, without the distractions of differences between nationality or background, to focus on individual differences. In what follows I give a brief indication of the variety of activities, materials, methods and approaches that we used, none of themselves new, but all of which contributed to a greater investment on the part of both teacher and learner.

NEEDS AND WANTS

The first line of action identified above was to make negotiation central to the way the course was run

One of the ways in which we sought to achieve this was to spend a substantial amount of class time discussing the rationale underlying the course syllabus, the timetable balance and our methodology. If the students made a convincing case for change, we adjusted the programme. There were other consequences too: we had created the perfect context for students who were feeling demotivated, to develop effective presentation and negotiating skills, one of the aims of the course. We were also observing different personalities with different ambitions emerging.

The second line of action was matching materials to learner characteristics

This involved timetable changes too, to allow for less lock-step work; it also involved a move towards workshops and small-group teaching. To give a few examples: in the Writing Workshop students were encouraged to bring relevant non-private correspondence: we were quickly dealing with invitations from tutors, letters from TV rental firms, and junk mail of all sorts. Any articles about Taiwan, identified by student or tutor, were pinned up on the notice board and often used in the class on Language and the Press. In the Grammar Workshop we used the work of past course members to encourage the students to become aware of typical Chinese mistakes. Groups were sometimes ridiculously unbalanced as far as numbers were concerned, but reflected student interest and allowed the tutors to choose the right material: a text book for two, authentic materials for nine. It is very easy in EAP/ESP to lose the respect and the interest of the students as they begin to struggle with their subject specific academic classes. Tailoring the content of the language classes to the students' interests avoided this problem and allowed us to get to know more about the students as individuals.

The third line of action was to identify attitudes, beliefs and goals

We had already created an interest and a need for this by our flexible and consultative approach. We needed, however, to be reminded that the students' attitudes to teaching and learning made them find our approach confusing and unsettling. By giving them freedom, we had attacked their sense of security. Cultural awareness was crucial for both sides: we had a weekly session on Intercultural Relations which looked both at the theory and the students' own experiences. We used Horwitz' Beliefs About Language Learning Inventory (BALLI) with great success. The inventory asks for an opinion on five major areas: aptitude, difficulty of language learning, nature of language learning, communication strategies and motivation. Again we learned about each other's point of view. As well as adding to our repertoire of tasks we learned to allow for different pathways through the tasks: cooperative (our preference) and competitive (their preference). We accepted that students set themselves different targets and challenges: one is desperate to move into a 'higher' group, another prefers to stay 'down' with friends. One writes an essay based on already acquired knowledge, another uses the opportunity to research a new topic; one writes a succinct and clear account; another will produce a detailed and well-illustrated one. One student even 'bought' himself out of the Presentation Skills class since he saw a greater need to spend time on writing essays, and signed a contract to this effect. In these attempts to understand each student as an individual with a highly complex set of motivations we were trying to translate individuality into a productive force in the learning group. We were also trying to use an increase in learner participation and responsibility for what goes on in the classroom as an important motivational strategy (c.f. Hotho-Jackson 1995).

Strategies and study competences

The threefold division of learning strategies proposed by O'Malley et al, already mentioned earlier, usefully brings together in one framework a hierarchy of competences that successful learners need to develop. Metacognitive strategies function as higher-order and more general strategies which are more pervasive and organizational in influence e.g. advanced organizers, directed attention, self-monitoring, self-evaluation (ibid.). They serve to give direction to other strategies and need to be developed as study competences. Cognitive strategies, in contrast, concern more specific behaviours which are themselves linked to more circumscribed learning situations e.g. reordering or reclassifying the material to be learned; using target language reference materials; consciously applying rules to produce or understand the second language (ibid.). These are closer to study skills. Underlying both sets of strategies is not only the need to develop Waters and Waters' ideal student, but one who is linguistically aware.

Indeed the underlying focus behind each language class was language awareness. A knowledge of how language works is crucial for noticing the different linguistic devices used to encode different purposes and attitudes. By dint of awareness activities and discovery techniques the students became much better at linguistic analysis. They became interested in information structure, in lexical choice and its syntactic consequences. They began to understand point of view and irony. They were able to monitor their own production.

The third set of strategies, social strategies such as cooperation, are really only hinted at in O'Malley. Oxford (1990) builds on his work and identifies: asking questions (e.g. asking for clarification or verification); cooperating with others (e.g. proficient users of the new language); empathizing with others (e.g. developing cultural understanding). Within the classroom these were relatively easy to develop. A range of teaching modes, a channel for negotiation, individual consultation time, were all in place. Outside the classroom personality and cultural attitudes came into play, making each individual's use of such strategies unpredictable and idiosyncratic.

Assessment

This is in some sense where we started. Marks and grades usually imply a standard - which the student may have failed to reach, and may not even have wanted to reach. Students often continue to get the same range of grades for the course, as tutors' expectations of them rise; they therefore find it difficult to believe they have made progress. We needed a system that would balance academic expectations with a form of assessment which would allow each student to evaluate their progress in terms of their own aims: whether it was increased accuracy or social skills, or a greater understanding of European politics or of British Soaps. In other fields, 'life experience' is given credit. The student who joins ten societies and is out with native speakers every evening, may have a more effective learning strategy than the student who stays in to study, even though he does not hand in his assignment on time. We tried to give value to such outside learning experiences, in our written reports and in the way we dealt with individual students in class. At the same time we included some normative assessments, not least to fulfil the sponsors' requirements. The initial IELTS scores were a useful diagnostic tool; the bi-termly tests on grammar, vocabulary, reading and listening were a way of identifying gaps in ability that might otherwise have been overlooked; the presence of an external assessor, for the end of term presentations and the long essay, made it possible to judge both personal successes and targets met, as well as more objective progress. In some cases these grades clearly reflected sustained linguistic progress; in other cases, though hard work and commitment to the course were not in doubt, weak students were consistently labelled weak; in yet others, students who had 'slept' through much of the course were rewarded with above average grades. The self-evaluations from the students, the tutors' comments on individual projects and the feedback from one to one tutorials told a different, if sometimes complementary, story. The overall picture was necessarily complex, but revealed what we intended - the range of individual differences.

CONCLUSION

An approach which requires constant adaptation and fine-tuning is demanding for the tutors and potentially confusing for the students. The rewards are worth the risk. There are gains on a personal level and on a professional level for all the participants. Discussion (often metalinguistic), negotiation, and presentation skills are quite naturally given an authentic and important role in the class. A developing awareness, for both teachers and students, of the relatavism of pedagogic values leads on to broader cultural understanding. By reflecting on the assumptions underlying their practice the teachers discover new and successful ways of teaching. The students experience directly the Western concern for the individual and for democratic decision making. This focus on the individuality of the students, and on their interests and achievements outside the classroom as well as their linguistic success, encourages the 'weaker' students and allows the 'demotivated' students to find new reasons for taking active part in the learning process. These students will not necessarily get high grades, but they will not have been labelled as failures. They will have learnt respect for themselves and for their teachers.

REFERENCES

Hotho-Jackson S. (1995) 'Motivation and group context: tackling the drop-out factor'. *Language Learning Journal* 11.

Horwitz E. (1987) 'Surveying student beliefs about language learning' in Wenden A. and J. Rubin *Learner Strategies in Language Learning.* Prentice-Hall International.

O'Malley J. et al. (1985) 'Learning strategies used by beginning and intermediate ESL students'. *Language Learning* 35:21-46.

Oxford R. (1990) *Language Learning Strategies: what every teacher should know.* Newbury House.

Richards J. and C. Lochart. (1994) *Reflective Teaching in Second Language Classrooms.* CUP.

Skehan P. (1989) *Individual Differences in Second-Language Learning.* Arnold.
Waters M. and A. Waters. (1992) 'Study skills and study competence: getting the priorities right.' *ELT Journal* 46/3: 264-273.

Peer Support Through Shared Learning Experience in an Essay Writing Task

Susan Vincent

My search for a new approach to teaching essay writing in the EAP classroom was prompted by a growing dissatisfaction with the results of using an approach which was too product orientated and maintained a highly teacher-centred attitude to error correction and learner feedback. Over the years I have developed a keen awareness that the students themselves were a potential teaching/learning resource which was being wasted, and that their knowledge and skills should be recognised and valued.

In this respect, peer support offers learning strategies which encourage self and peer appraisal, and enables students to identify personal strengths and weaknesses and develop models of good practice through a shared learning experience.

In this paper, I describe and evaluate a writing programme based on the idea of shared learning. In this programme Students on ERASMUS programmes at Middlesex University Business School were asked to prepare for their coursework assignment - an essay writing task - through a programme of shared learning. French students were required to write their essay in English, British students to write in French. The essay writing process was carried out through pair work and a planned programme which defined specific stages of activities,

Firstly, I will consider the theoretical background to the programme of shared learning in the writing process. I then give a summary of the total process of the shared learning experience and finally consider how peer support can develop capability and improve language competence.

PROCESS AND PRODUCT

It must be assumed that the long term aim of our EAP students is to satisfactorily complete their course of study with evidence of having produced the required written assignments and of having achieved the desired grades. Thus, implicitly, EAP must be concerned with product.

Traditionally, the provision of a model in teaching has been seen as crucial. The emphasis has been placed on correctness whether of language structure, rhetorical functions or cohesive devices: the concern is with the organisation of ideas and the use of form. This is understandable with the stringent conventions regarding the expression of ideas in British essay writing. However, Flowers and Hayes (1977) and others have criticised these model-based approaches as being inhibiting.

With the recognition of the importance of fluency along with the communicative approach in ELT - with language teaching focusing on the learner writer's purpose and on what they want to say - a new procedural model (sometimes referred to as the Deep End Strategy) was put forward White (1990). This advocated five main stages:

- a focus on the task
- an attempt at communication as far as possible
- reference to a given model which is not to be imitated but used as a resource
- practise as necessary
- recycling.

In recent years, EAP teachers of writing have adopted techniques which were developed for native speakers. ELT researchers in writing, such as Freedman, Pringle and Yalden (1983), and Zamel (1984), have showed that the development of the writing skills of native English speakers has relevance for the non-native speaker. Thus, the development of second language writing is seen as an on-going *process* of enquiry and adaptation based on the belief that education is a journey of discovery rather than simply the achievement of predicted outcomes (White (1990)). It also recognises that writing involves cognitive processes which are cyclical and recursive.

PEER REVIEW

Peer review is a fundamental part of the process approach. It comprises students reading each other's drafts and suggesting possible revisions. Mittan (1989) and others have shown peer review to be a powerful learning tool. Mittan pointed out that peer review provided an authentic reader; it increased student's motivation for carrying out the writing task; it provided the opportunity to receive different views; it helped students to view their own writing critically; and it aided them in gaining confidence. Mangelsdorf (1992) writes of similar findings.

Peer review has been referred to in many ways: for example, peer response, peer editing, peer feedback, peer correction. Each name conjures up a particular slant or function. I have chosen to use the term 'peer support'.

PEER SUPPORT

Peer support follows the student right through the whole process to completion of the final product - the finished essay. It includes peer response at the start of the process which concentrates on the development of ideas and organisation; peer feedback, as the form and arguments of the essay develop; and peer editing with attention to grammar, spelling, punctuation. In addition, peer support also depends on collaboration and negotiation with students deciding together what comments to give and how to express them.

I mentioned above my dissatisfaction with using conventional error correction whether it be 'full correction', 'controlled' or 'notation'. Witbeck (1976) is sceptical that an error corrected in one context could be transferred to the elimination of similar errors in other contexts without a two-way discussion of the problem. Zamel (1985) suggests that conventional error correction cannot deal with problems in organising a cohesive text. In any case, it is a time-consuming ordeal for the teacher and perturbing for the learner to see an array of comments that may well contribute to the learner's lack of confidence. It militates against writer autonomy when students should be given opportunities for editing and proof reading their own texts. However, peer support can offer a healthy learning environment for formative feedback (correction) during the drafting process and thereby reduce the amount of 'error correction' by the teacher in their assessment of the submitted essay.

ESSAY WRITING - A SHARED LEARNING EXPERIENCE

This section gives an account of the programme of learning comprising peer support in an essay writing task. It starts by explaining the situation and context in which the programme took place. It then describes the programme the students followed and concludes by outlining the outcomes, benefits and potential pitfalls of such a programme.

Situation and context

Twenty French and twenty British students were on an ERASMUS exchange programme in the first year of a joint course leading to a BA in European Management from Middlesex University and the equivalent DESEM qualification from the business school in Marseilles.

Both the French teacher, teaching French for Academic Purposes (FAP) to the British students, and myself, teaching EAP to the French students, felt we had a resource in the students which was under valued and also that they had little opportunity to get to know each other. This provided the initial stimulus for drawing up this programme of learning.

The programme

At the start of the programme students were already receiving input and taking part in workshop activities on the conventions of British essay writing: for example, analyzing the essay task/question; paragraph layout; avoiding direct questions; and using logical connectors (see Appendix).

In the first session, we began by bringing together the French and English students and giving each student a copy of the programme pack in the target language. The purpose of the programme was explained and discussed with the students. They were then asked to form pairs - one French, one British - bearing in mind it was easier to work with someone with whom they feel comfortable and with whom it would be convenient to work, such as another student living in the same locality.

Each student was then asked to consider the four essay writing tasks, each relating to a different topical or cultural issue of the country of the target language. For example:

- So notorious is British pollution that the 'Dirty Man of Europe' tag has been reserved for us alone by our continental neighbours". What evidence is there to support this view and how far is it justified?

Each student was asked to choose one essay task. It was important that the subject or theme of the essay chosen appealed to both students.

The following describes the programme as presented to the French students with its various stages.

AIM

To promote cooperation between yourself and your partner for the benefit of your learning, and to develop a critical approach to your use of language through the preparation and writing of an essay.

OBJECTIVES

1. To heighten awareness of the influence of culture in language learning.
2. To develop your vocabulary, an appropriate essay style, and your use of grammar in the English language.
3. To practise British essay writing conventions previously taught in class.
4. To experience how learning from each other plays a valuable part in the learning process of each individual as well as in the product (essay).
5. To experience the usefulness of your peers as a primary resource and as a guide in the use of other learning resources.
6. To help you reflect more constructively and to develop a more critical approach to your work through peer assessment.

(Each pair was asked to arrange to meet at regular intervals in their own time to carry out the various stages in the process of the essay writing).

MEETING 1 (week 1)

Purpose

1. To discuss the vocabulary likely to be needed in the essay: a maximum of 20 words related to the essay topic.
2. To discuss possible content of your essay - key ideas, evidence, examples
3. To discuss possible source material.

Action

To write up a draft **introduction** and the **main concepts** (paragraphs) of your essay.

MEETING 2 (week 3)

Purpose

1. To discuss each other's draft introduction and paragraphs.
2. To offer comment and feedback for improvement with reference to established reference criteria

Action

Write a draft of your essay. Give this to your partner during week 5 so s/he can prepare to give you feedback in week 6.

MEETING 3 (WEEK 6)

Purpose

- To bring to the meeting the drafts of the essays.
- To discuss the comments and notes for feedback marked on your essay paper so that you can gain ideas for improvement of your writing.

Action

Write the final version of your essay in the light of the comments.

OUTCOMES

1. An increased cross-cultural awareness of both individual and institutional issues.
2. Improved competence in your use of English concerning vocabulary development, grammar, appropriate style and register.
3. An understanding of the difference in the conventions of French and English essay writing, and your demonstration of this in your essay writing.
4. The improved production of effective coherent discourse in your essay writing. This involves the sequencing and linking of ideas between paragraphs and sentences.
5. The ability to reflect more constructively and critically on your work.

PEER SUPPORT

Problems

On the whole, we underestimated the adjustment that students from a different learning background would have to make - from a more teacher-directed approach to student centred activity. The carefully structured programme of meetings was obviously crucial. Negative comments from the students revealed that some of their partners were too vague and came to meetings poorly prepared. It is interesting to note that similar problems are mentioned by Mangelsdorf (1992). Students expressed the view that the option of attending tutorials during the process would have helped them through problems which arose.

Benefits

The following points summarise the main positive elements of peer support.

- It is a useful vehicle for reflection concerning the significance of cultural issues and the use of the language in writing.
- It takes into account student knowledge and skills: it does not deny them but gives them value.
- The learner can feel free to take risks and explore during the process of writing. This is enhanced when there is a good relationship with the partner.
- It recognises the need for learners to contribute and to express views which leads to an increase in confidence and the ability to receive counter opinions constructively.

- It draws on the benefits of extra knowledge which differences in experience and world knowledge have to offer.

Student support takes into account both surface learning and deep learning. In the former, the student takes what s/he learns and adds it to their store of unconnected facts. In the latter, the student makes sense of ideas and concepts; this involves thinking, seeking and playing with ideas.

In this 'shared learning experience' part of peer support involved peer assessment. In this context, peer assessment did not involve students acquiring marks but students making qualitative judgements. The following table shows how peer support brings a second dimension to assessment.

Two orientations of assessment

Student-centred	*Teacher-centred*
Process	Product
Formative	Summative
Evaluation focus	Grading focus
Intrinsic value to self	Extrinsic value to self
Motivating - carrot	Motivating - stick
Promotes enquiry	Cue-seeking
Criterion-referred	Norm-referred
Enabling - values success	Critical – identifies failure
Relative - improvement effort	Absolute - external standards
Time / place - flexible	Time / place - fixed

(Adapted: Chris Osborne, Middlesex University, 1993)

CONCLUSION

It seems that peer support has the potential to heighten students' awareness of the process component of learning (skills and competencies) as well as the product component. It provides the opportunity for developing autonomy and personal responsibility in learning. The benefits of peer support may not simply be apparent in the production of a well prepared essay, but have long-term implications for both students and staff.

ACKNOWLEDGMENT

The author wishes to thank Josette Rees-Smith, Senior Lecturer in French, Middlesex University for her collaboration in this programme of peer support.

REFERENCES

Flowers, L.S. and Hayes, J.R. (1977) 'Problem-solving strategies and the writing process', *College English*, 39 (4): 449-461.

Freedman, A., Pringle, I. & Yalden, J. (Eds.) (1983) 'Learning to Write: First Language/ Second Language', Longman.
Mangelsdorf, K. (1992) 'Peer reviews in the ESL composition classroom: what do the students think?' *ELT Journal*, 46 (3): 274-284.
Mittan, R. (1989) 'The Peer Review Process: Harnessing Students' Communicative Power', in Johnson and Roen (Eds.) '*Richness in Writing: Empowering ESL Students*', New York, Longman: 207-219 .
White, R. V. (1988) 'Academic writing: Process and product', in Robinson, P. (Ed.) *ELT Documents* No.129, Basingstoke, Modern English Publications in association with The British Council.
Witbeck, M. C. (1976) Peer Correction Procedures for Intermediate and Advanced ESL Composition Lessons', *TESOL Quarterly*, 10 (3): 321-326.
Zamel, V. (1984) 'In search of the key: research and practice in composition', in '*On TESOL '83, The Question of Control*', Washington, D.C.: TESOL.
Zamel, V. (1985) 'Responding to Student Writing', *TESOL Quarterly*, 19 (1): 17-37.

APPENDIX

INTRODUCTION TO THE ESSAY

Interpretation of title and introduction

DEVELOPMENT OF THE ESSAY

Logical development
Content relevance
Use of sources
Use of evidence
Understanding of topic
Development of argument

CONCLUSION TO THE ESSAY

OTHER FEATURES

Fluency
Use of grammar
Use of vocabulary
Spelling
Punctuation

(Adapted from Brown, S. et al. 'Strategies for Diversifying Assessment in Higher Education', Oxford Centre for Staff Development).

How to REAPE the Benefits of Study Skills Courses: Embedding EAP Within Real English (RE)

Damian McDevitt
INSET, Botswana

For many years now language teachers have been aware of the dangers of assuming that a heavy focus on form will necessarily lead to accurate grammatical production: knowledge of the rules about language cannot be equated with ability to use language. Although this is a truism for most EFL teachers today, EAP teachers seem to have failed to recognise the same problem in a different guise. Study Skills courses often focus on EAP competence, that is knowledge about the rules and format of academic writing, but fail to develop EAP performance. This article will look at a typical approach to the teaching of two essential skills in EAP writing, viz. referencing and essay planning, and see how far they fall short of achieving their objectives.

Research suggests that students score better in EAP writing tests if the tests are based on familiar content.

> *The hypothesis was supported that students from a particular discipline would perform better in tests based on texts taken from their own subject discipline than would students from other disciplines. That is, students appear to be advantaged by taking a test on a text in a familiar content area.*
> *(Alderson & Urquhart, 1983)*

If this is true of testing, it is likely to be true also of teaching and learning; that is, EAP skills will be learnt more efficiently if they are based on familiar content. When we look at EAP course books however, we find that content is often given a very low priority, especially in the area of referencing and essay planning.

TRADITIONAL TARGET OF REFERENCING EXERCISES

Course books devote quite a lot of time to the mechanical aspects of using reference material within an essay, giving advice on such things as:

a) the layout of reference markers, e.g. (Peters, 1992)
b) the position of markers: do they appear before, after or in the middle of the quotation and what happens when the author's name has already been mentioned?

c) the importance of integrating a quotation into the student's own text and the need to add or subtract words (in the case of direct quotations) to achieve clarity and grammaticality.
d) the layout of the bibliography (alphabetical order, author's initials etc.)

On the other hand, they say very little about the process of what to select from the sources. This, in my opinion, is the crucial part of the skill. So often a student's reference is only loosely related to his/her point and neither clarifies, illustrates nor advances the particular argument. This kind of breakdown in coherence shows a major flaw in communication and is generally much more difficult to remedy than the mechanical defects that the course books seem to focus on.

ARTIFICIALITY OF EXERCISES

When we look in detail at some of the typical referencing exercises we can note a number of common failings. Firstly, there is often not enough prior text for the student to latch the reference material onto. This produces what I call the raindrop syndrome where a large globule of information hangs precariously by a very thin strand. The following example from Wallace's Study Skills in English (1984) illustrates this.

> *Below is a selection of quotations. Write them in the way that you would quote them, if you had occasion to do so. Follow the instructions carefully. There is an example to show you what to do, and some useful phrases at the end.*
>
> *Example. Quote what the author has to say about "the working class" in the United States.*
>
> *THE WORKING CLASS. The heads of families of this class frequently have not finished high school. They work steadily, in good times, at jobs that require little training and can be mastered in a few days or, at most, a few weeks. (Vance Packard: The Status Seekers, Longmans, 1960)*
>
> *Answer. Packard (1960) has this to say about the working class in the United States: "The heads of families of this class frequently have not finished high school. They work steadily, in good times, at jobs that require little training and can be mastered in a few days or, at most, a few weeks."*
>
> *Exercise 1. Quote what the author has to say about "the real upper class" in the United States.*
>
> *THE REAL UPPER CLASS. These are the people ...*

What students usually do is stick to the very safe but stilted rubric quoted in the example and produce five or six references all of which start:

> *Writer X has this to say about topic Y.*

In some cases the semantic content of course book exercises almost disappears. Take this example, quoted in full, from Jordan's Academic Writing course (1990) where the author is illustrating the use of quotation marks:

> *... (Seers, 1979), a further dimension is added – "development now implies, inter alia, reducing cultural dependence on one or more of the great powers." Self reliance thus becomes ...*

The second problem is that students have to work backwards from given knowledge to the unknown. The trick here lies in trying to glean enough information from the source material to guess at what was likely to have come before it. This hardly seems an appropriate strategy for developing logical coherence. Thirdly, longer assignments designed to test referencing skills start from the source itself. So for example, we ask our students to write an essay on "The Breakdown of Marriage in Society" and supply them with two or three pages of "stimulus" material from the *Education Guardian.* The whole exercise is top heavy with the result that the source controls the topic rather than the other way round. It is hardly surprising then that as markers, we find ourselves writing comments like, *This is very derivative or You stick very closely to your source material.*

REAL REFERENCING

Finally, if we look closely at real examples of referencing as used by **real** writers, we will notice some further discrepancies. Firstly, the ratio of text to reference material is on a rough average 2:1 - that is, two thirds of a paragraph is taken up with the writer's presentation of an idea and one third with the reference which supports it. If we look at many of the models given in course books, this ratio is inverted (c.f. the example from Wallace quoted earlier).

Secondly, if we examine the function of real world references we note that they all serve to illustrate, clarify or support the writer's point of view (or occasionally an opposing point of view) but they are never used to introduce completely new information. This unfortunately is not the case with course book exercises. Quite often the information presented in the source material is the only information that the student has on the topic. Not surprisingly then, it becomes quite difficult for the student to present the reference material as subordinate to or supportive of his/her argument.

The third point relates to a discourse pattern (statement > support > restatement) visible in many types of communication, and not unlike the "initiation > response > feedback pattern in classroom discourse (Ellis, 1995). In real world references, a writer will present an idea, develop it by reference to other works, then redirect the reader back into his own line of thought. The following extract from Rivers (1989) illustrates this three part pattern:

> *Motivated use, where students talk about things they really want to talk about is not being tapped, as it must be if language is to be learned for actual communication, rather than as communication in the abstract. We may be getting closer to communicative competence, but we are still in the realm of demonstrations of acquired competence, rather than genuine performance.* ***"Usage,"*** *says Widdowson,* ***"is ... that aspect [of performance] which makes evident the extent to which the language user demonstrates his knowledge of linguistic rules. Use is another aspect of performance: that which makes***

> ***evident the extent to which the language user demonstrates his ability to use his knowledge of linguistic rules for effective communication"*** *(1978) Demonstrating the ability to use, no matter how artfully the opportunities for demonstration are contrived (through role playing or simulated situations, or whatever), is not use. Real use can occur only in episodes of effective communication -student-originated and student-sustained. Here the idiosyncratic and unpredictable will inevitably intervene, despite the best-laid schemes of materials developers and classroom teachers. This is genuine interaction.*
>
> (My bold to highlight stages of the discourse)

Many course book examples end abruptly after the source material and there is no redirection to the writer's argument.

ESSAY PLANNING

If we now turn to another important element in study skills, viz. essay planning, we can again see that they often fall short of realistic practice. In particular, many exercises simply make the task too easy.

A common type of exercise is that of selecting / organising ideas to give practice in drawing up essay plans. Thus, for example, students may be required to choose from a given list of points about a proposed site for a new University, then group them under four main headings. This exercise offers a short cut to get the students started on the selection / organisation process, but it is precisely the part which is cut out that is the most valuable element of the task. Students efforts to produce these initial ideas themselves can be tortuously slow and what is often referred to in the course books as brainstorming more aptly resembles damp drizzle.

The second problem is that text book ideas for this type of exercise are too neatly packaged and bear little resemblance to what the students produce, if given a free hand. It overlooks the crucial value of concise formulation in essay planning.

Two areas which students frequently find difficult when drawing up essay plans are:

a) the amount of information in each point: achieving the right balance between whole sentences (unwieldy and too final) and cryptic clues (with virtually no meaning) is a skill which needs constant practice.

b) correct formulation of headings and sub-headings, so that the student (and teacher) can easily verify that what follows is indeed in the right place. Correct formulation is often the key to meaningful classification. We have all been guilty of making those "slight adjustments" to student suggestions when drawing up a blackboard plan. The following are examples from a plan for an essay entitled "Women's Development in the Third World".

Student formulation	*Teacher formulation*
Women must know to cook, clean, be educated	Improvements in home management
Too many children for development	Need for family planning

Unless we can get students to express their ideas concisely and meaningfully, they are always going to have serious problems of organisation and coherence.

CONCLUSION

So far I have highlighted a number of weaknesses in typical study skills courses, but have not offered any solutions. It is my belief that we must develop EAP courses which grow out of content courses and are carefully linked to them, rather than starting from contrived sets of data. Whether the content refers to bona fide common ground (as often happens with pre-sessional courses) or to degree-related requirements (e.g. that all first year students follow a 20th Century Britain course) is immaterial. The essential point is that all students should have access to familiar content which they have already had to grapple with outside the EAP classroom and which can be used as the raw material for study skills development. Such a basis can, I believe, help in three ways: it can reduce the problem of mental block (especially getting started), it can allow students to practice genuine study skills without getting bogged down in comprehension issues, and it can give them some of the subject labels which will help in the formulation of their ideas. It is time for EAP teachers to have a serious look at the content of their discipline.

REFERENCES

Alderson J. And Urquart A. (1983) 'The Effect of student background discipline on comprehension: a pilot study' in Porter D. And Hughes A. (eds.) *Current Developments in Language Testing* (Academic Press).

Ellis R. (1987) *Understanding Second Language Acquisition* (OUP).

Jordan R.R (1990) *Academic Writing Course* (Nelson).

Rivers W. (1989) *Communicating Naturally in a Second Language* (CUP).

Wallace M.J. (1984) *Study Skills in English* (CUP).

Widdowson H (1978) *Teaching Language as Communication* (OUP).

Why Don't They Say Anything: Investigating the Participatory Environment on Postgraduate Courses

Barbara Thornton
University of Leicester

INTRODUCTION

As postgraduate degrees grow in popularity, participants on such courses are becoming increasingly diversified in terms of cultural, educational and linguistic backgrounds. Where much of the input on such courses is learner-centred this can lead to difficulties in ensuring that all students are involved in all activities. At best, the result may be very mixed levels of engagement with those participating least being viewed as not particularly useful members of the group; at worst it can lead to underlying feelings of antagonism and frustration or a split within the group into those who do participate and those who are perceived not to "pull their weight".

Often these feelings remain latent. In recent years, students on the MA course in Applied Linguistics and Teaching English to Speakers of Other Languages (TESOL) at Leicester University have been keen to articulate concerns over the impact of teaching styles on relationships within a group. On speaking to colleagues from other departments, it was apparent that the problem was not confined to those studying TESOL. This paper describes an attempt to investigate such issues on post-graduate courses across a limited range of disciplines by looking at factors which may affect degrees of participation.

This is a small scale study based on:

- observation of "seminars" in the departments of Mass Communication, Management and Applied Linguistics / TESOL
- semi-structured interviews with teachers and students
- a questionnaire administered to 47 postgraduate students (21 native speakers and 25 non-native speakers

Such a study will inevitably yield only partial insights and no claims are made for the generalisability of findings, but nevertheless it does signal a number of areas which may be of interest and worthy of further investigation.

INVESTIGATING PARTICIPATORY ENVIRONMENTS

Seminars are frequently cited as the main arena in which students need to exercise their speaking skills. However, when one examines the range of events which have been described as seminars, the difficulty of preparing students for such a latitude of encounters becomes apparent. The three events we observed, all of which were termed seminars for timetable purposes took very different forms:

Seminar 1

The topic of the seminar was introduced by the tutor, after which three students read previously prepared papers. Each paper was followed by a student initiated discussion phase. (Mass Communication - 8 students)

Seminar 2

All students had read papers prior to the seminar. The tutor then set key questions of a problem-solving nature for consideration first of all in pairs, then fours, then in larger groups. (Applied Linguistics - 13 students)

Seminar 3

This seminar actually consisted of an interactive lecture by the tutor, followed by two fifteen minute oral presentations by students. The students' presentations were followed by a discussion phase orchestrated by the tutor. Students were evaluated on their presentations including their ability to deal with questions. These evaluations formed 10% of their final grade for the course. (Management - 26 students)

We decided to video seminars 1 and 3 having weighed up the advantages of having "realistic" data against the disadvantages of the disrupting effects of the camera. Students in Mass Communication were, in any case, used to being videoed and it was felt that the presence of a video camera would not significantly affect the interaction. Filming seminar 2 where so much of the communication was in small groups was felt to be inappropriate and instead, three observers took notes focusing on levels of participation of a range of students within the group.

After each seminar, all the students were asked to fill out a questionnaire which focused on their feelings about the seminar, their own behaviour in it and their perceptions of its success. They were also asked what tutors could do in order to improve the effectiveness of the event as a learning experience for all students. A Likert type scale was used to measure their levels of anxiety in a number of academic speaking situations. Selected students were interviewed about their perceptions of the success of the event and their own participation in it.

WHAT DETERMINES DEGREE OF PARTICIPATION?

It was possible to make the following generalisations based on findings from all three methods of data collection.

1. Age

Brumfit (1993) makes the point that overseas learners of English in British universities are usually older and more experienced than home students. It is certainly true that a wide range in age is a feature of many masters courses. It was therefore interesting that age and experience were mentioned by several students as playing a part in levels of participation with one student firmly placing this as the most important variable determining levels of oral contribution.

> *... the age differential is something of a feature on a master course - there tends to be quite a wide age difference as well and some of the younger students will feel a bit shy or inhibited and I think it didn't matter whether they were home or overseas students - it's the age and experience more than anything.* (African student, Mass Communication)

It is interesting to speculate on the link between this view and the country of origin. If learners come from a culture where wisdom based on age and experience are valued, they might feel more able to share those experiences with others in seminar discussions.

2. Gender

Gender has long been recognised as a factor in levels of participation across a range of educational contexts. In higher education, Hutchinson and Beadle (1992) quote research which demonstrates clearly that teachers call on male students more frequently than female students. Furthermore, male students tend to be asked questions which require deeper level, critical thinking whereas females are often only asked simpler factual questions. Because female students are given fewer opportunities for meaningful interaction, they are less confident in their classroom talk and have lower expectations of their own performance. Hutchinson and Beadle (1992) conclude that "*despite gains women have made in higher education, many mixed-sex classrooms still have environments that discourage participation by women". This was an area commented on by a German female student after the Mass Communication seminar.*"

> *"I noticed the girls didn't speak much. It's mostly the men".*

On analysing the video of this seminar, we found that all five men spoke on more than one occasion, while of the three women one did not speak at all, one spoke only briefly when called on by name by the lecturer. The only woman to contribute significantly was an international student actually presenting a paper. However, while she was able to answer questions on her own paper in a clear and articulate way, she took no part in the discussion of the other papers during the seminar.

Similar findings were repeated in the other seminars. During the early interactive phase of the Management Seminar, only males asked questions of the lecturer and only males responded to open solicits from him. In the remainder of the seminar, the only questions initiated by women (two NNS, one NS) were addressed to the female student presenter and were supportive rather than information seeking in character. Likewise in the larger group discussions which were a feature of the Applied Linguistics seminars, males spoke more often and for longer than females.

3. Language level and native speakerness

It is obvious both from common sense and the research literature that linguistic ability is, to some degree, bound to affect academic success (Blue, 1993, Grundy,1993). It was therefore surprising to find, from our interviews and questionnaires so few references to the role of language in determining the degree of participation. Although one student, on being paired with a NS did comment that she

> *...did not like being asked to discuss with a native speaker because I do not speak English so well* (Non-native speaker Applied Linguistics)

this may be more to do with levels of self-confidence rather than with language ability. During our observations, only one instance was observed when a non-native speaker tried to make herself heard and could not, where this might be ascribed to the fact that she did not possess the necessary linguistic strategies for interrupting.

The Mass Communication seminar was dominated by two males - one a native speaker, the other with near native proficiency. The most frequent contributors to the Management seminars were likewise native or near native males. Within the Applied Linguistics seminar, it was generally true that while levels of participation in pair work were generally well balanced, native speakers did dominate as groups increased in size (as measured both by number of turns and total speaking time). In post-seminar discussions, there was on occasions speculation as to whether this could be partly attributed to personality.

However, there were marked differences between the perceptions of NS and NNS when it came to judging their own performance in seminars. While 15 of the 21 native speaker students felt comfortable with their level of participation, claiming they had spoken as much as they wanted to, for non-native speakers this figure was much less with only eight students (all male) who were happy with their level of participation. One student commented:

> *I spoke as much as I wanted to and as much as I could, but I know I should speak more.*

This pressure to speak led to strategies such as rehearsal of contributions reported by two non-native speakers and "speaking to fill the silence" reported by a non-native speaker who expressed considerable frustration with her silent peers.

4. Group size

The seminar with the least participatory activity was the management seminar where only nine of the twenty six students present contributed to the discussion. The fact that this seminar was held in a tiered lecture theatre where participants on occasions had to turn round to talk to each other may also have contributed to the low level of participation.

Group size is also a factor and the bigger the group the more uneven the interaction. The Applied Linguistics seminar we observed consisted of a pyramid discussion which yielded particularly interesting information as to the effect of size and composition of the group on patterns of interaction.

> *... it was interesting to see how well the group activities worked in twosomes but how pressure of time and larger groupings created tension and the*

> *withdrawal of many of the members actively taking part* (Native speaker observer)

The climate during the pair work stage was comfortable and relaxed. As the groups grew in size, the atmosphere became gradually more threatening as pressure was applied for completion of the large group task. Here normally prominent speakers asserted control, taking on the role of directive organisation handlers, demanding decisions and achieving strategies for resolution. At this stage, some students became marginalised or began marginalising themselves. This was evidenced in withdrawal from the group in terms of non-participation and body language.

> *...some students began to sit back even normally assertive types like X.* (native speaker)

> *...sometimes some people just seemed to manipulate the activity.* (non-native speaker)

The general consensus was that the larger the group, the more difficult it was to make contributions.

> *It was interesting to see how well the group activities worked in twosomes but how larger groupings created tension and the withdrawal of many of the members taking part.* (Native speaker observer)

One non-native student commented:

> *I did not feel comfortable in the large group so I did not speak a word.*

This bears out a number of studies showing that the larger the group, the less involved students are in discussion. Meredith (1987) found that atmosphere (as measured in terms of cohesion between students) is directly influenced by the size of the group. Mullen et al. (1989) reviewed eight studies dealing with seminars and found that as the group got larger, the dissatisfaction of group members increased.

5. Cultural considerations

Problems may also arise because of differing sociocultural expectations resulting in mismatched expectations of what behaviour is appropriate in academic discussions (Jin and Cortazzi 1993, Cortazzi and Jin, 1996). Thorp (1991) speaks of the "*invisible culture of the academic classroom*" and highlights the importance of "*knowing not only how to listen and taken notes, but also to* ***show*** *that one is listening*". In our observations, we noted one particular example of a student who did not participate at all and to our cultural eyes looked bored but who was nevertheless quite clearly following the discussion as evidenced by the way he took notes at key stages of another student's presentation. If such students appear (in the view of students and tutor) to fail to be attentive, it is unlikely that opportunities for participation will come their way. The negative mismatch can work both ways with students viewing tutors as lacking in knowledge while tutors view students as passive if not lazy. One native speaker student in Management reflected the strength of negative feeling towards these non-contributors:

> *grades should be given for participation in seminars so that the lazy ones are forced to speak.*

6. Communication apprehension

Communication apprehension (CA) is a component of language anxiety which has received attention in other second language acquisition (SLA) contexts (Gardner and MacIntyre,1993). CA is a broadly based anxiety related to oral communication defined as an "*individual's level of fear and anxiety which is associated with either real or anticipated communication*" (Daly and McCroskey 1984). While a certain amount of apprehension can enhance performance if the anxiety becomes too debilitating, the result may be panic, disorganisation and a generally poor speaking performance. Furthermore, when an excess of such fear is present, the individual may tend towards communication avoidance or withdrawal. Communication avoidance may be evidenced by, for example, students seating themselves where they feel they will not be called upon to speak or by skipping classes which they know will be discussion-based, a behaviour commented on by one of our lecturer respondents. Communication withdrawal is evidenced by speaking only the absolute minimum required, so, for example, speaking in class only when called upon by name or in dyadic interaction only answering questions or agreeing with the speaker. Again, this behaviour was typical of a number of students in our sample.

Research indicates that certain features of a situation will tend to increase anxiety levels regardless of personality type. Buss (1980) has identified several of these all of which could be found in one or more of our seminars. For example, the degree of attention from others will affect the level of CA. One non-native speaker reported how nervous she felt when everyone looked at her because she "*spoke with a foreign accent*". This consciousness of accent heightened the sense of unwanted, negative prominence that some people may wish to avoid.

A further example given by Buss is unfamiliarity which can relate to situation, people or task. If students are unfamiliar with exactly what is required, they will tend to be more anxious. For example, at one level, a student stated that she was worried whether the clothes she was wearing were appropriate for a seminar presentation. Another student was unsure about the type of question it was appropriate to raise in a seminar. Although it is true that feelings of unfamiliarity with higher education contexts may fade, this may happen at different rates for different students. If tutors familiarise students with expectations and make these explicit, then anxiety should be lessened.

A significant number of students in our sample reported degrees of shyness about speaking, stating this as a reason for low participation.

> *The feeling of being "English-shy" sometimes attacked me during the pyramid group activity.* (non-native speaker, Applied Linguistics)

This bears out Jordan's (1989) view that it may be lack of confidence rather than linguistic or sociocultural difficulties which prevent a student from contributing to discussions.

However, while a degree of shyness was reported by students of all nationalities, when asked to rank their levels of anxiety in various academic speaking situations, NNS experienced significantly higher levels of CA when engaged in both pair and group discussion, indicating that even this type of interaction was stressful for many students. Levels of anxiety when presenting papers were equally high for home and international students

> *...native speakers find presentations difficult as well and need training.* (NS Mass Communication)

IMPLICATIONS

1. Furneaux et al (1991) note the importance of finding out exactly what constitutes a seminar within a particular department and feeding this information into pre-sessional course design. It is all too easy to take good practice for granted. Even with our limited study, we found, for example that one department encouraged the students to present in seminars by reading previously scripted papers, a method we had actively discouraged on our pre-sessional course. Students need to be made aware of exactly what is expected particularly in formal situations where behaviour is highly prescribed.

2. The linguistic and sociocultural aspects of seminar skills also need to be more closely based on what actually happens, so that in terms of language as Lynch and Anderson (1991) note what is taught is actually what is used in the seminar room. There may also be a place for skills not traditionally taught such as active listening, showing supportiveness and questioning techniques.

3. If native and non-native speakers find presentations difficult, there may be a case for doing joint sessions in this area. As one student remarked:

   > *We need proper training in how to do presentations, rather than just the odd hint here or there.* (NS Management)

4. When asked what tutors could do to ensure that the seminar was a positive learning experience for all, a number of students focused on the facilitative role of the tutor who was felt to bear the major responsibility for the success of the seminar. Tutors were encouraged to ensure even participation by controlling dominant students and by using nomination strategies to ensure contributions by all.

5. Observation of the individual can help to highlight any imbalances in participation due to gender or nationality. One observation we conducted identified the fact that the tutor had a strong pull to one side of the classroom, favouring students sitting in that area. Often such awareness raising is all it takes for the tutor to take necessary action.

6. If as this preliminary research suggests, anxiety is an issue, then this too is an area which tutors need to address. Research in other contexts seems to indicate that skills training in itself is not enough. Greater skill does not necessarily mean less anxiety. Here the EAP tutor might look towards some of the techniques from neuro-linguistic programming (NLP) which is finding its way into the fringes of general ELT. (Revell and Norman 1977). For example, often students think they are going to perform badly and therefore do - the self-fulfilling prophecy. NLP reframing exercises focus on changing the students'

cognitive appraisal of their own abilities. Students are taught to manage their own self-evaluation and develop more facilitating self-talk. Other techniques provide individuals with the insights into the unproductive thinking that induces their anxiety.

CONCLUSION

Participation in academic discussions is an area of difficulty for many of our students even after a period of time in the country. As Jordan (1997) points out the problem is that students just don't participate. Traditional seminar skills training as practised on our own pre-sessional course seems to have a limited effect. Only a larger-scale study with a more balanced sample will show whether the reasons we have identified hold true more generally. Once we know why levels of participation are uneven, we can look in a more principled way at redressing the imbalance and helping our students.

REFERENCES

Blue G (1993) 'Nothing Succeeds Like Linguistic Competence: The Role of Language in Academic Success', *Language, Learning and Success: Studying Through English*, Modern English Publications / The British Council

Brumfit C (1993) 'Culture and Success' in Blue (ed) *Language, Learning and Success: Studying Through English*, Modern English Publications / The British Council

Buss A H (1980) *Self-Consciousness and Social Anxiety*, Freeman

Cortazzi,M. and Jin, L. (1993), Cultural orientation and academic language use in Graddol, D., Thompson, L and Byram, M (eds) *Language and Culture* 84 - 97, Clevedon, Avon: Multilingual Matters

Cortazzi, M and Jin, L.(1996), Cultures of learning: language classrooms in China in Coleman, H. (ed.) *Society and the Language Classroom,* 169 - 207, Cambridge: Cambridge University Press

Daly J A and McCroskey J C eds (1984) *Avoiding Communication: Shyness, Reticence and Communication Apprehension* Sage Publications

Furneaux C Locke C Robinson P Tonkyn A (1991) 'Talking Heads and Shifting Bottoms: The Ethnography of Academic Seminars' in Adams P Heaton B Howarth P (eds) *Socio-Cultural Issues in English for Academic Purposes* Modern English Publications / The British Council

Gardner R C MacIntyre P D (1993) 'A Student's Contribution to Second Language Learning, Part 2: Affective Variables' *Language Teaching* 26 1-11

Grundy P (1993) 'Student and Superviser Perceptions of the Role of English in Academic Success' in Blue (ed) *Language Learning and Success: Studying Through English* Modern English Publications / British Council

Hutchinson L Beadle M (1992) 'Professors' Communication Styles: how they influence male and female seminar participants' *Teaching and Teacher Education* vol 8 no 4 405-418

Jordan, R.R (1997), *English for Academic Purposes,* Cambridge: Cambridge University Press

Lynch T Anderson K (1991) 'Do you mind if I come in here? A comparison of EAP seminar / discussion materials and the characteristics of real academic interaction' in Adams P Heaton B Howarth P (eds) *Socio-Cultural Issues In English for Academic Purposes* Modern English Publications / The British Council

Some Different Expectations of a Selection of Pre-sessional EAP Projects

Catherine Montgomery and Linda Pearsall
University of Essex

This article reports on a small research project which considered a selection of pre-sessional EAP Projects. The aim of the study was to compare feedback on the projects from EAP tutors and subject tutors with a view to developing assessment criteria which would be valid in terms of pre-sessional requirements and expectations of receiving departments within the university. Three academic areas were chosen; Economics, Linguistics and Accounting and Financial Management (AFM). Eight projects from each discipline were sent out to the relevant departments and subject tutors were asked to make a comment on each one. These comments were then compared with the comments made at the end of the pre-sessional course by EAP tutors. There was considerable variation in the comments particularly regarding the projects which required analysis of the subject. The findings suggest that more awareness of the written work priorities of particular departments would improve EAP tutors' ability to provide EAP students with the correct expectations for what is required of them by their departments.

INTRODUCTION

The project is a major element in the September module of the pre-sessional course at Essex. Until 1994 students were grouped roughly according to levels of ability for all aspects of the course. Students worked on projects individually and presented their work in an oral presentation as well as in written form. While students found the opportunity to practise seminar skills in this way very useful, they found it difficult to remain interested in detailed information from other subject areas.

In 1994 organisational changes were made and students were grouped in two ways: according to language level for language improvement and study skills development; according to subject area for project work. In addition students were encouraged to work in groups of two or three (although those interested in a highly specialised area could work individually). The project also involved three, rather than two areas of study and preparation: a written piece of work, an oral presentation and a poster presentation showing a summary of the students' work. Departmental staff from the different subject areas were invited to attend the poster presentations to meet their prospective students and to discuss their areas of interest. The presentations were very successful and departmental staff indicated the usefulness of meeting overseas students before the beginning of the academic year.

We felt the changes made were an improvement but we also felt they needed monitoring particularly in relation to preparation for EAP staff whose role on the project changed from that of supervising students with a variety of specialist backgrounds to that of working with students in a specific subject area. Since we had also developed closer links with other departments it seemed an opportune time to consider the parity of expectations of all those involved: the students, the EAP tutors and the subject staff.

We looked at three specific subject areas: Linguistics, Economics and AFM and examined feedback from EAP tutors and subject tutors on students' written work. A selection of eight projects for each subject was sent out to the three departments mentioned and subject tutors were asked to make a comment on each one. These comments were then compared with comments made by EAP tutors at the end of the pre-sessional course. The following data shows the types of comments tutors made and how positive or negative they were.

METHOD OF COMPARISON

It was clear from reading the comments that there were distinct differences. Thus the following method of categorising the comments was designed in order to quantify these differences. Firstly, a general assessment was made as to whether the comments were negative or positive; a scale of 1-5 was created to represent the range of comments made and this was as follows:

1 = Very Positive e.g. Excellent
2 = Positive e.g. Good
3 = Quite Positive e.g. Some good points
4 = Fairly Negative e.g. bad
5 = Very Negative e.g. poor

Secondly, the type or area of the comment was focused on. For quantification the following five areas were found to cover all types of comments made:

1: Grammar and Language (including expression of ideas)
2: Subject Matter
3: Structure (arrangement, development, introduction and conclusion, coherence cohesion)
4: Academic Presentation (references, sources, bibliography)
5: Effort of student

In addition to this the projects themselves were divided into two rough areas according to whether the piece was a description of a subject or whether an analysis was required. Titles and content were carefully considered and a decision was made as to whether the project required an analysis, that is whether the student had to consider the implications of the information s/he was presenting, or whether it was simply necessary to present or describe information. In some cases an analysis was actually required but none was given (one subject tutor openly commented on this) and these projects were classified as analyses. This was, in fact, a simple approach to a very complex issue; the concept of genre and argument classification is a research field in itself (Johns:1988 and Swales:1984 are just two examples of discussion and research in this field) and deserves more consideration than it has received here. However, this rough division provided an interesting aspect to the consideration of the data in this study.

EXPLANATION OF THE DATA

Turning to the comments themselves, findings are explained here by department so that comparisons can be drawn across academic fields as well as between EAP and Subject tutors.

A. Economics

First, the general attitude of the comments on each project (positive or negative) was considered.

Figure 1. Positive or Negative Comments Compared with Essay Type

Project and Type	*Subject Tutor*	*EAP Tutor*
A: (analysis)	4	1
B: (description)	2	3
C: (description)	2	2
D: (analysis)	4	1
E: (analysis)	3	1
F: (description)	2	3
G: (description)	2	2
H: (analysis)	3	1

Key: 1 = Very Positive e.g. Excellent; 2 = Positive e.g. Good; 3 = Quite Positive e.g. Some good points; 4 = Fairly Negative e.g. bad; 5 = Very Negative e.g. poor

Figure 1 shows the raw numbers of responses (the sample of data was considered too small to justify the application of statistical analyses such as a Chi-square). As mentioned above, there was noticeable variation in the subject and EAP tutors' perception of how successful the projects were and upon closer examination this variation appeared to be related to the type of project in question. There were an equal number of description and analysis projects and the description type projects showed the most consistent remarks; projects B, C, F and G all received similar comments from the EAP tutors and the subject tutor. These descriptive projects were fairly positively assessed by both the subject tutor and the EAP tutor although in two cases the EAP tutor was slightly less enthusiastic.

The projects which had been labelled analyses, however, produced quite different assessments. Projects A, D, E and H were the ones the tutors disagreed about most. These analysis projects were more negatively assessed by the subject tutor but positively assessed by the EAP tutor.

Secondly, the types of comment made were considered (Figure 2).

Figure 2. Type of Comments

Project and Type	*Subject Tutor*	*EAP Tutor*
A: (analysis)	2,3	1,3,5
B: (description)	2,	1,3,4,5
C: (description)	2,1,3,	3,2,
D: (description)	2,3,	5,3,4,1,
E: (analysis)	2,1	1,2,3,4,5,
F: (description)	1,2,	3,1
G: (description)	5,2,4	4,3,1,2
H: (analysis)	5,2,1	3,4,1

Key:1: Grammar and Language (including expression of ideas); 2: Subject Matter; 3: Structure (arrangement, development, introduction and conclusion, coherence, cohesion); 4: Academic Presentation (references, sources, bibliography); 5: Effort of student

It was found that the subject tutor commented most frequently on subject but also commented in four out of eight cases on language and on structure three out of eight times.

The EAP tutor focused most on language and structure. S/he also, however, commented frequently on academic presentation and effort and three out of eight comments included mention of the subject matter.

B. Linguistics

The projects in the field of Linguistics were examined in the same way. Firstly the positive or negative attitude of the tutor was guaged (Figure 3).

Figure 3. Positive or Negative Comments Compared with Essay Type

Project and Type	*Subject Tutor*	*EAP Tutor*
A: (description)	4	4
B: (analysis)	3	1
C: (analysis)	4	1
D: (description)	3	2
E: (description)	2	2
F: (description)	2	2
G: (description)	2	1
H: (description)	1	1

Key: 1 = Very Positive e.g. Excellent; 2 = Positive e.g. Good; 3 = Quite Positive e.g. Some good points; 4 = Fairly Negative e.g. bad; 5 = Very Negative e.g. poor

In this case there were more description projects than analyses (only two analysis types) but as with Economics, the description projects showed the most consistent marks. Projects A,D,E,F,G and H all received similar levels of positive or negative comments from the EAP tutors and the subject tutor. Again, the descriptive projects were positively assessed by the subject tutor but less positively seen by the EAP tutor.

The analysis type projects as before produced very varied assessments. Projects B and C were the ones the tutors disagreed most about. The analysis projects were again more negatively assessed by the subject tutor but positively assessed by the EAP tutor.

Secondly, the types of comments were examined.

Figure 4. Type of Comments

Project and Type	*Subject Tutor*	*AP Tutor*
A: (description)	2,3,4	1,3,
B: (analysis)	4,3	4,1,3,2
C: (analysis)	3.4	4,3,2
D: (description)	1,	4,3,1
E: (description)	5,4,	3,4,1,
F: (description)	4,2,	1,4,
G: (description)	1,2	3,4
H: (description)	3,2,5	5,4

Key: 1: Grammar and Language (including expression of ideas); 2: Subject Matter; 3: Structure (arrangement, development, introduction and conclusion, coherence, cohesion); 4: Academic Presentation (references, sources, bibliography, including comments like 'well-researched', 'academic style'); 5: Effort of student

The Subject tutor commented most frequently on Academic Presentation and secondly emphasised subject and structure.

The EAP tutor also commented most frequently on Academic Presentation and then structure and language. It was interesting to note that s/he also commented twice on subject matter.

C. Accounting and financial management

As with Economics and Linguistics the positive or negative nature of the comments was considered first.

The descriptive projects showed fairly consistent assessment by both EAP and subject tutors. There was also some consistency with the analysis type projects: A,F, and H received similar comments. In D however, the subject tutor commented mainly on lack of extended prose which inhibited the expression of ideas to the extent of excluding any comment on subject matter. The EAP tutor on the other hand, thought it well argued and readable.

As shown in Figure 6, the subject tutor commented in seven out of eight projects on subject area and structure, but also in five out of eight on grammar and language.

The EAP tutor focused most on grammar and language, eight out of eight, and also commented frequently on structure and student effort. Four out of eight comments included mention of the subject matter.

Figure 5. Positive or Negative Comments Compared with Essay Type

Project and Type	*Subject Tutor*	*EAP Tutor*
A: (analysis)	2	2
B: (description)	4	3
C: (description)	4	3
D: (analysis)	4	2
E: (description)	3	4
F: (analysis)	2	2
G: (analysis)	2	3
H: (analysis)	2	1

Key: 1 = Very Positive e.g. Excellent; 2 = Positive e.g. Good; 3 = Quite Positive e.g. Some good points; 4 = Fairly Negative e.g. bad; 5 = Very Negative e.g. poor

The type of comments made by both tutors on the AFM projects were then focused on.

Figure 6. Type of Comments

Project and Type	*Subject Tutor*	*EAP Tutor*
A: (analysis)	1,2,3	1,2,3
B: (description)	2,3	1,2,3
C: (description)	1,2,3,4	1,2,3
D: (analysis)	1,3	1,3
E: (description)	1,2,3	1,5
F: (analysis)	1,2,3	1,5
G: (analysis)	2,3	1,2,3
H: (analysis)	2	1,5

Key: 1: Grammar and Language (including expression of ideas); 2: Subject Matter; 3: Structure (arrangement, development, introduction and conclusion, coherence, cohesion);4: Academic Presentation (references, sources, bibliography, including comments like 'well-researched', 'academic style'); 5: Effort of student

SUMMARY AND COMMENT ON THE COMPARISONS

1. Differing expectations: process or product

In both Economics and Linguistics the EAP tutors were generally much more positive about the projects than the Subject tutors. In AFM the EAP tutor was slightly more positive, but comments were generally not as positive as in Economics or Linguistics.

As EAP tutors have knowledge of the students and their work and also try to give encouragement, they prefer to emphasise the process students are going through in producing the project and are likely to be more positive in their feedback. Subject tutors are more objective in their assessment of the end product as they had no knowledge of the student and were unconcerned with the process students had gone through. Having said this, it was interesting to note that subject tutors in some cases did make comments on effort (as in

Economics in figure 2) which suggests that it may be possible to consider effort without having witnessed the process of producing a piece of work.

The positiveness of the EAP feedback could, however, be misleading for students in that they could perceive it as a sign that their project may be used as a model for work in their academic department or that their Academic English or their approach to it needs no further improvement. In particular EAP tutors made comments relating to the actual "success" of the final product of the project and this could be an area for concern as the dangers of a mismatch in expectations are quite real and have been discussed in a number of recent studies; for example, Thorp (1991) points out 'a student's idea of the nature of the essay will influence the questions he or she asks (or omits to ask) before tackling it.' Thus it is important that a student is not misled in his or her perception of what is expected by the process comments or final assessments of a pre-sessional project.

2. Differing expectations: analysis or description

In both Economics and Linguistics the analysis projects were quite negatively perceived and assessed by the subject tutor but were positively perceived by the EAP tutor and they produced the most disagreement between the two tutors. The description projects produced much closer assessments and tutors tended to agree on the descriptions in these two subject areas. In AFM, however, there were more analysis type projects, but assessments by both EAP and subject tutors were generally quite similar.

EAP tutors in this sample appeared to value the idea of including some sort of analysis in projects but because of lack of background knowledge in the subject were unable to identify whether the analysis was well-directed and accurate or not. Subject tutors, however, seemed to prefer an essay which required a simple description to an analysis which is not correct or fully explained. Descriptive essays tended to be much 'safer' in that tutors agreed much more on the assessment. In AFM the EAP tutor had an educational background in the subject which may account for greater parity in assessment and there being not such high scores for positive or negative comments. It is difficult to make too many assumptions on such a small sample, but this raises the well discussed issue of whether EAP tutors should comment on subject content or not and whether or not it is possible to assess the value of an analysis or description without having background knowledge.

3. Differing expectations: type of comment

The Linguistics projects produced more similar types of comments, with both tutors commenting frequently on Academic Presentation and structure. The Economics projects however, produced quite different types of comments from the two tutors, with the subject tutor quite predictably commenting most on the subject matter (this fits in with Weir's (1988) study on what subject tutors prioritise) and the EAP tutor again predictably commenting most on structure and language. The Economics subject tutor interestingly did comment in four out of the eight cases on the language and grammar of the projects and the EAP tutor made three out of eight comments on the subject matter of the projects. In AFM high priority was given by the subject tutor to both subject and structure. The Subject tutor in AFM pointed out that a post-graduate course requires much more use of argument type of essay writing not simply of analysis of data. Therefore the ability to write extended, coherent prose is essential.

EAP tutors who assessed the Linguistics and AFM projects had more background knowledge about the subject than the tutors assessing the Economics projects and this could account for the fact that their assessments were closer in type to the subject tutor although there was still disagreement over the Linguistics' analysis type of writing. It is interesting to note that both subject and EAP tutors assessing the Linguistics projects appeared to value academic presentation and structure quite highly. The AFM and Economics subject tutors made a number of comments on language and grammar and the AFM subject tutor also focused on structure. This raises the issue of how much value in terms of assessment should be given to the ability to write well-structured, 'academically fluent' pieces of writing and how much to actual coverage of content (cf. Thompson, 1995). This issue may have become more significant over the past five years as there has been considerable discussion as to whether the general and academic competence of students being admitted to university departments has decreased. Concern over language and structure issues may have developed due to this, contradicting Weir's (1988) statement that we should be less concerned with accuracy of language and grammar.

At Essex, the expectation of the AFM tutor with regard to the value of the project on the pre-sessional course is to prepare students to write a well-structured and fluent essay. The tutor does not see the role of the project as giving the students the opportunity to analyse data as there is a departmental introduction to analysis of statistics. This may conflict with EAP tutors' expectations of what they should be preparing students to do in a subject such as AFM.

IMPLICATIONS AND RECOMMENDATIONS

As mentioned at the beginning of this article, the purpose of this research was to establish realistic criteria for assessment of pre-sessional projects at Essex. Below are some suggestions for methods of utilising the information found here and also some recommendations for further research.

It would be useful and informative to build up a bank of responses from tutors in different departments (cf. the approach of Horowitz, 1986) detailing what they consider to be important in written assignments (our experience of the differing expectations of subject and EAP tutors in the area of AFM underlines this need). Ideally, it would be worth collecting a number of responses from each department and dividing the comments into graduate and undergraduate tutors' expectations. The replies could be used to brief EAP tutors prior to working on pre-sessional Projects with students.

Given the variation in type of comments by EAP tutors, it would be useful to design a set of detailed guidelines for EAP tutors to follow when giving oral and written feedback on the Projects both during the course and when the final written project is completed. (These guidelines may vary according to the academic area for which the project is being written). This would increase the possibility of EAP tutors giving students more realistic expectations of what is required by their department.

The study which has been described here was an attempt to make the nature of the pre-sessional project more valid by establishing further details of expectations and priorities for written work in three academic disciplines. It was useful to consider exactly what is expected of a student working on a pre-sessional Project. This appears to be to encourage the student to analyse the culture and discourse community of the academic situation they are about to enter and to increase students' awareness of the writing conventions, topic choices and types of descriptions and analyses they are going to have to produce (Johns, 1988). Because an academic discourse community is never static it is important that research in this area remains a constant concern so that the expectations of students, EAP tutors and subject tutors can be as closely linked as possible.

REFERENCES

Horowitz, D.M. (1986) What Professors Actually Require: Academic Tasks for the ESL Classroom. *TESOL Quarterly*, Vol 20, No 3. Sept.

Johns, A. (1988) The Discourse Communities Dilemma: Identifying Transferable Skills for the Academic Milieu. *ESP Journal*, Vol 7. No 1.

McKenna, E. (1987) Preparing Foreign Students to Enter Discourse Communities in the US. *ESP Journal*, Vol.6, pp187-202.

Swales, J.M. (1984). Research into the structure of introductions to journal articles and its application to the teaching of academic writing. In R. Williams and J. Swales (Eds.), Common Ground: *Shared interests in ESP and Communication Studies*, (pp. 77-86). Oxford Pergamon Press in Association with The British Council.

Thompson, G. (1995) Language Problems in Assessments: a Query. *IELTDHE Newsletter*, Vol 3.1, Jan.

Thorp, D. (1991) Confused encounters: differing expectations in the EAP classroom. *ELT Journal* Vol. 45/2. April.

Weir, C. (1988). Academic Writing - Can we please all the people all the time? In *Academic Writing: Process and Product*. ELT Documents 129. Modern English Publications in association with The British Council.

Are We Teaching the Right Words? A Study of Students' Receptive Knowledge of Two Types of Vocabulary: "Subtechnical" and "Technical"

Jiawei Liu and Hailary Nesi
Centre for English Language Teacher Education, University of Warwick

INTRODUCTION

The study described in this paper was motivated by concern to identify the English language learning needs of postgraduate students of Engineering from Hong Kong and Malaysia at Warwick University. When a sample of these students were interviewed informally to find out more about their language problems, they revealed that they were experiencing difficulties with technical terms, rather than with other types of vocabulary.

This information seemed to conflict with the received wisdom of EAP, which identifies subtechnical rather than technical vocabulary as problematic for learners studying in the medium of English at tertiary level. Such learners will already have acquired a broad base of general English words during their secondary education, and it is claimed that they can learn technical terms directly from their subject tutors and textbooks (Kennedy and Bolitho, 1984, Higgins, 1985, Nation, 1990). This leaves a middle category of words to be taught in EAP classes: a category, however, which is not well-defined in the EAP literature.

Our study set out in the first instance to define the categories of technical and subtechnical more precisely, and in ways that did not rely solely on the intuition of the EAP practitioner. It then aimed to identify the words in these two categories which our Engineering students would need to know, and to investigate more fully our students' claims that they needed support with the acquisition of technical rather than subtechnical words.

SUBTECHNICAL AND TECHNICAL WORDS

Although most writers seem to agree that EAP teachers should concentrate on vocabulary that is neither technical or general, the choice of words to fit this category varies. Widdowson (1983), for example, emphasises the importance to EAP of "procedural vocabulary": discourse-organising words which have little meaning outside the text, but which are used to structure the information carried by more topic-specific (technical) lexis. This emphasis is echoed by Baker (1988), and King (1989) in their descriptions of subtechnical vocabulary. Higgins (1985), on the other hand, includes topic-specific items such as *boil, heat* and *chemicals* in his list of "frame" words to be taught in the EAP class; his choice is largely based on their perceived difficulty for EAP students. A different approach again is taken by

Kennedy and Bolitho (1984); they focus on vocabulary which also occurs in general English, but acquires a different meaning within an academic context. These words, like those identified by Higgins, are chosen for the EAP syllabus because they are thought to create particular difficulties for learners.

Farrell (1990) offers a more easily quantifiable definition of subtechnical vocabulary. He defined the subtechnical words in his 20,000 word corpus of texts on Electronics as "those formal, context-independent words with a high frequency and/or wide range of occurrence across scientific disciplines, not usually found in basic General English courses". Farrell's definition is useful for its emphasis on the objective facts of word frequency and range; unlike some of the approaches mentioned above, it does not rely on intuition or personal judgement. The definition is somewhat misleading, however, because it does not seem to regard frequency and range as two independent parameters, but rather as alternatives (he writes of "high frequency *and/or* wide range").

Yang's criteria of frequency and range (1986) is preferable in this respect. In Yang's corpus-based study "subtechnical" words were those with high distribution across a range of fields, whereas "technical" words had a peak distribution in one particular field. In the study reported in this paper Yang's criteria were used as the primary means of categorising words.

THE CREATION OF TECHNICAL AND SUBTECHNICAL WORD LISTS

Having decided on our criteria for identifying technical and subtechnical words, we developed a corpus of Engineering texts so that we could identify the words in these two categories which our Engineering students would encounter in their studies.

Twenty-six modules are taught on the MSc Engineering programme at Warwick University, so twenty-six texts were selected to represent them. The texts were taken from highly recommended textbooks on the programme reading list. Each text contained roughly 8,000 running items, resulting in a corpus of 197,485 running words.

From this corpus we derived a list of 9,979 word types. We eliminated from this list those types that were amongst the 5000 most frequent in General English, according to Thorndike and Lorge (1944), because our students had a good grounding in General English and were likely to know most of these words. (We had previously tested the general vocabulary knowledge of a sample of nineteen postgraduate Engineering students from Hong Kong, and had found that at the time of their enrolment at Warwick their mean score on Nation's Vocabulary levels test at the 5,000 level (Nation 1990) was 82% (s.d. 17.21)).

4,981 of the 5,000 most frequent words in Thorndike and Lorge's list occurred in the corpus; accounting for 170,228 tokens (82% of the corpus). About half of these tokens were grammatical words.

Technical words were defined as those words on our list that had a low distribution and a frequency of five or more occurrences within the sample for a particular module (see Tables One and Two). The lowest distribution was one, meaning that the word occurred in the sample for only one module. This was the commonest distribution for technical words; 342 out of 668 occurred with this distributional range. Words with a higher distribution were also defined as technical, however, if they occurred with peak frequency in only one sample. For example, "simulation" occurred 40 times across 5 modules; but with a distributional pattern of 1, 1, 2, 3, and 33.

In addition to single-word items, we also identified a number of multi-word items identifiable as technical words on the basis of their distributional patterns. For example, "polyvinyl chloride" was considered a technical word because the two component words co-occurred 15 times in only one text. Similarly the compound "polyphenylene oxide" occurred 11 times, and "shear strength" 10 times, both with a distribution of one.

Table 1 shows the very low distribution of technical terms in the text sample for the module *Polymer Materials, Processes and Products.*

Table 1. A sample of technical words from the module *Polymer Materials Processes and Products*

	Frequency	*Range*
polymer	106	1
molecule	21	1
thermoplastics	19	1
polyester	18	1
polyethylene	16	1
polypropylene	15	1
polystyrene	11	1
polycarbonate	9	1
polyamide	7	1
polyurethane	6	1

Table 2 shows a different distributional pattern for technical words in the module *Quality Reliability Maintenance Systems.* In Table 2 "reliability", "probability", "maintainability", "warranty", and "mean time between failures" had a much higher distribution than one, but their distribution peaked in one text only, and they only occurred once or twice in each of the other texts. For this reason they were classed as technical rather than subtechnical words.

Table 2. A sample of technical words from the module *Quality Reliability Maintenance Systems*

	Frequency	*Range*
reliability	154	8
probability	19	4
failure rate	17	1
maintainability	11	2
warranty	10	3
hazard	10	1
mean time between failures	10	2
repairable system	10	1
life cycle cost	5	1
rate of occurrence of failures	5	1

About 8% of running words in the corpus were classed as technical by this means.

Having eliminated from our list those words that were also frequent in general English texts, and identified technical words, we were left with two remaining types of word, low frequency items that occurred in only a small proportion of samples (words such as *unrehearsed, venturesome, whims, wrestling* and *yoghurt*, which made up 2% of the corpus) and relatively high frequency words that occurred across a relatively wide range of samples. The first category was ignored for the purposes of this study, but the second category constituted our subtechnical word list. Table Three contains a sample of these words.

Table 3. A sample of subtechnical words listed in order of frequency

	Frequency	*Range*
ensure	46	15
priority	45	16
precise	43	18
fundamental	42	17
conventional	42	15
assessment	42	12
external	41	10
negative	40	8
feasible	40	7
manual	39	15
context	38	13
formula	30	15
equivalent	30	9

346 word types were identified as subtechnical in our corpus, accounting for 7,777 tokens (4% of the corpus). These words tended to have a wide indexical range, and to have a procedural function in that their lexical realisation occurred within rather than outside the text (Winter 1977, Sinclair and Renouf 1988). For example some of our subtechnical words could be classified as Vocabulary Three (Winter 1977), because they functioned "as special signposts of what a sentence means in sequence with its adjoining sentences". *Equivalent* is a Vocabulary Three word because it can be used to mark a matching clause relation, whilst *assessment, negative,* and *feasible* can be used to mark the evaluation stage in a problem-solution text pattern. Moreover some nouns, such as *assessment, analogy, context, diagnosis, formula, perspective,* and *version*, functioned anaphorically (Francis 1986) in our corpus by summarising the information content of preceding text.

The study

Having identified 611 technical words and 346 subtechnical words which our students would encounter during their course of study, our next step was to test a sample of the student population to find out whether one of the two word categories was better known than the other.

We chose 50 MSc Engineering students as experimental subjects. 20 were from Hong Kong and 30 were from Malaysia. All of them had arrived in the UK at approximately the same time twelve months previously, and were tested when they were about to finish their course of study . This meant that they had all already had opportunities to encounter the vocabulary items we would use in our test, through their prescribed reading. Our subjects had received little if any direct English language support during their time in Britain.

We decided to test each subject's knowledge of 120 technical words and 120 subtechnical words. Because subtechnical words occurred across a wide range of module samples, the same 120 words were used with every subject in this part of the test. The words which were selected from the subtechnical list for use as test items were those with typical subtechnical characteristics: they all had a range of at least 5 and a frequency of at least 10, and their role in the texts was "procedural" or "discourse organising" (Widdowson 1983, McCarthy 1991).

The words for the technical part of the test, on the other hand, had to be selected according to the sub-specialisms of each experimental subject. Technical words had, by definition, a low distribution, and it would have been unfair to test subjects on their knowledge of words that did not occur in the course modules they had opted to study. We therefore selected ten technical words to represent each module, and tested each subject on words from each of the twelve modules which constituted the MSc course requirement.

Once again, words for this part of the test were selected for their typicality, or in other words their high frequency in a low range of texts. It was apparent, however, that several modules did not provide sufficient instances of typical technical words. For this reason the technical words selected to represent *Simulation of Production/Systems* and *Basic Computing*, for example, had a slightly higher distribution and a lower frequency in individual samples than the technical words for *Polymer Materials, Processes and Products*, and *Steel and its Heat Treatment.*

Although the subtechnical and technical words chosen as test items had clearly distinct distributional patterns across the corpus, both sets of words occurred with the same degree of frequency within the corpus as a whole.

A yes/no format was chosen for the test, because it could be administered very quickly, and did not incidentally test other language skills that did not directly concern us (such as reading comprehension and writing). The subjects were presented with a list of words and asked to tick the ones they recognised. No dictionaries were allowed. Obviously, this format is vulnerable to cheating, because without built-in safeguards there will be nothing to prevent subjects from claiming that they know all the words presented to them. To prevent this from happening imaginary words were added to the authentic word list. This method had been used by Meara and Jones (1988) in testing non-native speaker students' vocabulary size. Subjects' scores were calculated taking into account the number of imaginary words each subject claimed to recognise. The formula proposed by Meara and Buxton (1987) was used to adjust the scores, but in fact little adjustment proved necessary, as there were remarkably few instances of "false alarms" in the data (only 6% of responses in the subtechnical vocabulary test and 7.7% of responses in the technical vocabulary test).

RESULTS

Table 4 presents the results of the vocabulary tests. It can be seen that subjects knew many more subtechnical than technical words. This difference was highly significant ($p < .01$)

Table 4. Comparison of subtechnical and technical scores

	Mean score	*SD*
subtechnical terms	94.29	8.42
technical terms	76.40	13.52

DISCUSSION

Our findings suggested that subtechnical vocabulary was more instantly recognisable to our subjects than technical vocabulary was. Our subjects did not appear to have acquired all the essential technical vocabulary through course work, in the manner proposed by Kennedy and Bolitho (1984), Nation (1990), Trimble (1985), and Robinson (1991), even though they were now at the end of their study period and were about to return to their countries of origin as qualified engineers.

These findings challenge received opinion regarding the type of vocabulary that needs to be tackled on an EAP programme. They suggest that the terminology traditionally dealt with solely in the subject specialism should be introduced, or at least reinforced, in the EAP classroom. This will not be welcome news for the majority of EAP practitioners, who often teach students from a variety of specialisms and sub-specialisms in the same class, and who regard themselves as linguists rather than terminologists. Before we make final decisions about the future content of our EAP syllabuses, however, two further issues need to be discussed.

Firstly, we must bear in mind that our findings do not necessarily reflect the vocabulary knowledge of the entire overseas student population. They probably have greater relevance for postgraduates than for undergraduates, because most postgraduate students already have a certain amount of experience of reading academic texts in English, and will have encountered subtechnical words across a range of fields in their undergraduate studies. This will give them an advantage in any subtechnical vocabulary test which undergraduate students will not share. Moreover, many postgraduate courses, like the Warwick MSc in Engineering, enrol students with backgrounds in a variety of subfields, and require participants to take modules in subfields that are new to them, as well as in subfields they have studied before. This means that at the start of the course all students will be familiar with the terminology of some modules but not of others. Whereas undergraduate students may be treated to a slow introduction to the terminology of their subject area, Masters degree students have only a few months to learn terminology which some of their fellow students already know.

Secondly, our vocabulary test was a receptive one; and words were presented without any surrounding context. Thus the results did not reflect subjects' ability to produce or interpret the two types of word appropriately in context. It may be argued that a contextual element is particularly important in the case of subtechnical items, because many have little or no meaning outside the text, serving a discourse-organising "procedural" function.. We do think it likely that a contextualised test would strongly confirm our initial findings, because context would aid recognition of procedural words more than it would aid the recognition of topic-specific words with extra-linguistic meaning. However, in future we will clearly need to examine in greater depth our subjects' knowledge of the two types of word used in context.

CONCLUSION

Our results suggest that postgraduate students from overseas have better knowledge of subtechnical vocabulary than technical vocabulary when they complete their course.

Future experiments of this type will need to investigate subjects' vocabulary knowledge at both the beginning and the end of their course of study, in order to ascertain the type and quantity of vocabulary acquired while studying in Britain. It may be that undergraduates' knowledge of the two types of vocabulary increases at an even pace over the extended degree period, while students on twelve-month postgraduate courses arrive with a good background in subtechnical vocabulary and acquire fewer new words while they are here.

If further studies confirm these initial findings, we will also need to investigate *why* otherwise successful students fail to learn terminology that is essential to a full understanding of their subject specialism. Is it because they lack the listening skills necessary to absorb oral definitions given during subject lectures? Is it perhaps because they lack strategies for interpreting glosses and definitions in subject textbooks? The answers to these questions may inform decisions on EAP syllabus design in the future.

REFERENCES

Farrell, P. (1990) Vocabulary in ESP: a lexical analysis of the English of Electronics and a study of semi-technical vocabulary. *CLCS Occasional Paper* 25 1-83

Francis, G. (1986) *Anaphoric Nouns* ELR Discourse Analysis Monograph. Birmingham: Birmingham University

Higgins, J. (1985) Hard facts (Notes on Teaching English to Science Students). in: Swales, J. (ed) *Episodes in ESP.* Oxford: Pergamon 28-34

Kennedy, C. and Bolitho, R. (1984) *English for Specific Purposes.* London: Macmillan.

McCarthy, M. (1991) *Discourse Analysis for Language Teachers* Cambridge: Cambridge University Press

Meara, P. and Buxton, B. (1987) An alternative to multiple choice tests. *Language Testing* 4 (2) 142-151

Meara, P. and Jones, G. (1988) Vocabulary size as a placement indicator in: Grunwell, P. (ed) *Applied Linguistics in Society.* London: CILT 80-87

Nation, P. (1990) *Teaching and Learning Vocabulary.* New York: Newbury House

Robinson, P. (1991) *ESP Today: A practitioner's guide.* Hemel Hempstead: Prentice Hall International.

Sinclair, J. and Renouf, A. (1988) A lexical syllabus for language teaching. in: R. Carter and M. McCarthy (eds) *Vocabulary and language teaching* 140-160 London: Longman

Thorndike, E. and Lorge, I. (1944) *The Teacher's Word Book of 30,000 Words.* New York: Teachers College, Columbia University.

Trimble, L. (1985) *English for Science and Technology: A Discourse Approach.* Cambridge: Cambridge University Press.

Widdowson, H. G. Learning Purpose and Language Use. Oxford: Oxford University Press.

Winter, E. (1977) A clause relational approach to English texts: a study of some predictive lexical items in written discourse. *Instructional Science* 6 1-92

Yang, H. (1986) A new technique for identifying scientific/technical terms and describing science texts. *Literary and Linguistic Computing* 1 (2) 93-103

Phraseological Standards in EAP

Peter Howarth
University of Leeds

INTRODUCTION

This paper presents a particular perspective on the differences between native and non-native academic writing: namely, the ways in which the two groups of writers deviate from expected norms in their use of collocations. It is too easily assumed that whatever native writers produce is correct or can be taken as a standard. For those interested in second language acquisition a close analysis of performance shows that the relationship between what native writers produce and what advanced learners write is more complex and more revealing.

Firstly, the paper will briefly review the theoretical framework within which the NS and NNS data will be described and identify what is regarded as significant in native writer performance and potentially problematic for learners' acquisition of collocations. Secondly, it will present a small amount of data from NS academic writing to illustrate how even proficient native writers may deviate from expected norms. Finally, it will examine NNS writing in order to draw comparisons and consider some implications for teaching.

PHRASEOLOGICAL COMPETENCE

It is, I believe, not uncommon for teachers of advanced EAP writing or subject lecturers reading the essays of overseas students to be confronted with instances of English of the following kind:

- *Most objections which assumed washback effects cannot be carried.*
- *Consequences ⇐ which bears very important influence upon the future of students.*
- *... that encourage somebody to pursue particular factors.*
- *Children adopt their natural tendencies to discover grammar.*

Writing such as this may pose problems for comprehension, might be regarded as non-standard English, yet is not ungrammatical (apart from minor lapses) and not easily accounted for by means of mainstream error analysis. The problem illustrated above arises from the co-occurrence of lexical items that do not form combinations that convey conventionally recognised meanings. They are regarded here as errors of phraseology, or phraseological deviations. Although competence in phraseology represents a high level of proficiency and errors such as these could be overlooked and might not even be noticed in certain contexts, for some purposes a higher level of phraseological performance is required. For translators and teachers accuracy and native-speaker naturalness are often demanded and phraseological conventionality is not to be regarded as an optional cosmetic layer of style.

For academic writers it is clarity of expression that is particularly valued, or, in any event, any lack of clarity should be deliberate and under the control of the writer. In non-native student essays lack of clarity may be noticed by EAP teachers or subject lecturers but is perhaps not generally attributed to a weakness in phraseological competence. The main reason for this is that phraseology has received very little attention in teacher training, and the situation is not helped by a lack of effective teaching materials that address the learners' difficulties. Too often materials writers concentrate on the apparent arbitrariness of collocation, which is of little use to teachers or learners in explaining the underlying nature of the phenomena or the causes of the problem.

DESCRIPTIVE MODELS OF PHRASEOLOGY

The model of collocation that is most familiar to teachers focuses on the co-occurrence of word forms on the surface of texts, and regards those that recur frequently as most significant in the language (see Sinclair, 1991): an approach that is well-suited to the automatic analysis of large bodies of text by computer. However, in order to understand the phraseological competence of second language learners, a model is needed that is capable of identifying and describing their performance in relation to native norms. Collocations occurring in texts are thus seen as realizations of lexical combinations that are stored by native speakers along with knowledge of complex phraseological features. This knowledge includes the crucial distinction between those combinations which are quite open and freely transformable (*carry a rabbit*) and those which are limited in their transformation or substitution, possessing, for example, restrictions on number (**on second thought*), on word order (**keep them under key and lock*) and on lexical substitution (**try more efforts*)[1].

The model that seems to offer teachers appropriate descriptive tools represents a continuum of restrictedness from those collocations that are entirely free to combine and recombine according to general semantic and syntactic rules to those that are quite fixed:

Table 1. Collocational continuum

free collocations	*restricted collocations*		*figurative idioms*	*pure idioms*
take learners *to language*	take refuge in *sth*	take a share in sth	*take sth on board*	*take part in sth*

This paper will not go into the details of the origins of this model on this occasion (see Howarth, 1993): a set of criteria can be established that will identify the relevant formal characteristics of collocations and distinguish between degrees of restrictedness. The central area of restricted collocation can be further subdivided in order to identify more precisely the very problematic borderline between this category and free collocations. The assumption

[1] The examples here are authentic non-native speech or writing.

is made that learners need most to know what is not free in word combinations (at what point they need to take into account knowledge about restrictions) rather than what is not idiomatic.

The application of this model is by no means straightforward, especially to large bodies of text, and very little of the analysis can be done automatically. It must be admitted that this analytical procedure works best on a small part of the whole spectrum of word combinations (those that are known as lexical collocations), and even among those the focus of the data presented here is narrowed to a few sub-categories: transitive verb + object patterns. However, in the language variety under discussion here these play a very important role in conveying the propositional content of an academic argument. Much of the procedural vocabulary of academic disciplines can be found in such predicate structures as *make a claim, reach a conclusion, adopt an approach, set out criteria.*

The value of this continuum model is that it can be related to several other features of interest to applied linguists, both formal and psychological, that are best seen in terms of gradience. Overall, these features can be seen as different dimensions of phraseological significance, is is important to note that significance bears no direct relation to frequency of occurrence as some interpretations of collocational significance suggest:

Table 2. Phraseological significance

phraseological significance is reflected in degrees of:
conventionality (institutionalization)
restrictedness (formal structure)
lexicalization (storage)
partial analysability (processing)

For the applied linguist or language teacher interested in understanding learners' phraseological errors, this model provides a framework for describing NS competence more precisely as the basis for describing NNS performance (and ultimately NNS competence). The data discussed here is taken from a large-scale study of academic writing that compared the production of non-native postgraduate students with that of native writers of social science texts. It is not suggested that there is a simple two-way opposition between the two groups of writers. A continuum could be drawn up to encompass mature NS writers at one extreme and weak NNS writers at the other, with NS and NNS students of varying levels of proficiency in between, and some overlap between native and non-native writers.

The NS data comprises two corpora:

- 29 social science texts from the LOB corpus totalling 58,000 words
- miscellaneous social science texts published by academic staff of Leeds University totalling 180,000 words

The NNS data consists of 10 postgraduate student essays on applied linguistics topics totalling 25,000 words. The students are teachers of English from Botswana, Burkina Faso, Germany, Greece, Hong Kong, Japan, Taiwan and Thailand, studying on an MA course in Linguistics and ELT.

NS DATA

The following examples, taken from the NS corpora, illustrate the application of the descriptive model and the resulting classification of collocations according to degrees of restrictedness. Within the central category of restricted collocations greater effort is required to differentiate between levels in order to understand more clearly the distinction between free and restricted collocations.

Table 3. Examples from NS data

Collocation	*Category*
COMPARE *behaviour, levels, results, size* EMPHASIZE *autonomy, concept, link, rights* INFLUENCE *content, culture, groups*	free collocation
SEE *need, value, opportunity, chance*	restricted collocation Level 1
INTRODUCE *bill, amendment, motion*	restricted collocation Level 2
MAKE *decision, improvements*	restricted collocation Level 3
PAY *attention, heed*	restricted collocation Level 4
GIVE *credit to, preference to*	restricted collocation Level 5
DRAW *a line*	figurative idiom
SET *store by*	pure idiom

At this relatively demanding level of performance it is clear from the data that NS writers deviate from expected norms on occasion. These occurrences are not remarkable in themselves, and might be dismissed as performance slips. However, it is the type of deviation that is of interest, and their significance lies in what they reveal about underlying processes. The framework enables one to pinpoint where along the continuum writers' competence seems to break down.

The number of deviant forms is, as one would expect, very small (<1%). Two main types of error have been identified. The first type relates to one of the most useful results of the detailed analysis, which has been to uncover certain clusters of overlapping collocations, found towards the free end of the restricted category:

Their significance lies in the way in which the analytical procedure helps to describe in great detail some of the combinations that are predicted by analogy, but arbitrarily blocked by usage, and clearly they are the kind of phenomenon likely to confound learners.

Table 4. Overlapping collocations

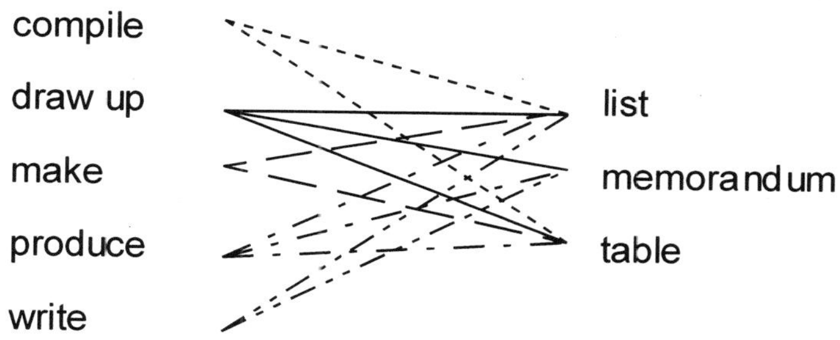

Native writers do not, on the whole, fall into the trap of producing collocations that are arbitrarily blocked. One of the very few in the data is:

> **concerning proposals done by historians*
> MAKE *a proposal*[2]
> MAKE/DO *a survey*

Most NS errors seem to occur towards the more restricted end of the continuum and many can be regarded as blends. The model suggests that these are the result of unconsciously merging two relatively strongly lexicalized collocations that would normally remain unanalysed in the writer's production. Some of these might pass unnoticed by the reader.

> **and we can pay particular care ⇐ to look at the fortunes of United Kingdom trade*
> PAY *attention*
> TAKE *care*

> **appropriate policy to be taken with regard to such inspections*
> TAKE *steps*
> ADOPT *a policy*

On the whole, however, NS academic writers, in the data examined in this study, are highly conformist in their use of collocations, appropriate to what could be called a convergent variety. This finding contributes to a greater understanding of what is often called an impersonal style. This conformity can be seen in terms of a convergence in style; a desire to co-operate with the needs of the reader, in contrast to the divergence that results from the creative manipulation of conventional expressions found, for example, in certain journalistic genres.

NNS DATA

The majority of NNS errors, on the other hand, seem to be the result of filling in gaps in clusters of overlapping collocations that are arbitrarily blocked.

> * *⇐ attempts and researches have been done by psychologist to find ⇐*

DO *a study*
MAKE *an attempt/a study*

**Those learners usually pay more efforts in adopting a new language by getting more contact* ⇐
PAY *attention/a call*
MAKE *a call/an effort*

**The learners may suffer difficulty in communicating in the target language*
SUFFER *pain*
EXPERIENCE *difficulty/pain*

As the overall figures bear out (and as one would expect), learners seem to be producing a greater proportion of their collocations by rule (free collocations) rather than from a stock of lexicalized combinations. Pawley and Syder in their 1983 paper make the important observation that

> Only a small proportion of the total set of grammatical sentences are nativelike in form.

Although in some circumstances teachers might applaud the willingness of learners to take risks with the resources of the language and experiment with novel combinations, by using more free collocations the NNS writer increases the opportunities for producing unconventional forms, which in academic genres can conflict with clarity.

The smaller number of fully lexicalized combinations (more highly restricted or idiomatic collocations) are perhaps produced more deliberately from a much smaller stock than a native writer has access to. They are probably learned as wholes and used largely correctly. The learners in the present study produced very few blends, and interestingly the clearest example comes from the most proficient writer in the group:

**If the students can achieve all the tasks with no difficulty* ⇐
ACHIEVE *goals*
PERFORM *tasks*

**We have drawn a favourable correlation between motivation and proficiency in language* ⇐
DRAW *a comparison*
MAKE *a correlation*

* ⇐ *emphasis will be given on the individual learners in relation to second language*
GIVE *weight to*
PLACE *emphasis on*

In one of the very few studies of this phenomenon, Dechert and Lennon puzzle over the occurrence of blends in the writing of their German subjects. They ask:

> why was it so full of collocational blends? ⇐ why, in spite of their many years of learning the language plus, in some cases, months of exposure to native speakers in England, had their apprehension of collocational affinities between lexical items not reached a state of proceduralized automaticity? (Dechert and Lennon, 1989)

There need be no great mystery. Blending is a sign of competence rather than incompetence and therefore an advanced type of error.

A question remains: Does it matter if learners produce such unconventional forms?

Pedagogically, there is a danger of overstating the case. Dechert and Lennon (1989), in their study of collocational blends in learner writing, regard the resulting errors as "peculiarly disturbing to the native-speaker reader. His awareness of the existing habitual collocations makes him quite unwilling and unable to regard this nonce collocation as acceptable". Korosadowicz-Struyñska (1980) is not quite so uncompromising and recognizes that "it is difficult to say ⇐ whether they [collocational errors] badly impair communication". She follows Johansson (1977), in suggesting a scale of error gravity, from the lowest grade to the highest; among the more serious errors are those errors in word collocations which "make the receiver tired or irritated or draw away his attention from the contents of the message" (Johansson). Cop (1988) refers to the 'discordance' caused by an 'infelicitous combination'.

Whether the eventual result is discordance, disturbance or irritation (rather too subjective to measure), these reactions are taken to be caused by the unaccustomed processing time and effort demanded of the reader, who is required to analyse into their component elements combinations that, when used conventionally, are only partially analysed.

It is not merely a matter of processing effort. If clarity of expression is regarded as a valuable property of academic writing, it may well be that there is a direct connection between clarity and conventionality. On the one hand, the use of conventional restricted collocations, or 'form-meaning pairings', can assist both writer and reader in successful communication. In production it is likely that the stock of conventional collocations such as *express a view, carry an obligation* or *obtain a result* helps the writer organize his/her thoughts. In the comprehension of the recurrent concepts and procedures of an academic discipline the occurrence of one element of a collocation will set up certain expectations in the reader's mind. The fulfilling of these expectations is clearly important for cohesion, but also has a positive psychological effect.

On the other hand, lack of clarity at a collocational level may be the result of a lack of clear thinking or understanding of the subject matter. Writers producing such combinations as

- *pursue a factor*
- *need a factor*
- *accomplish interest*
- *perceive information*

may not have succeeded in clarifying their own thoughts before attempting to verbalize them. Conversely, knowledge of a greater number of conventional collocations might assist them in the initial stage of clear thinking.

TEACHING COLLOCATIONS

This last point leads to the question of how knowledge of conventional collocations can be developed in learners. Leaving aside the very large issue of the place of collocational dictionaries in developing phraseological competence, it is informative to examine some of the teaching materials that are increasingly giving recognition to collocations. Unfortunately, however, the majority reveal a lack of understanding of what a significant collocation is from the point of view of language acquisition. It is a waste of time to give learners practice in producing combinations that, while institutionalized, are completely unrestricted and can be produced by the normal rules of English syntax and semantics. There is no need to give learners practice in producing combinations such as *eat a sandwich, ask a question* or *drink a cup of coffee*, at least not as collocations. There is, of course, an argument for teaching combinations that, while transparent within the semantics of English (intralingually), can pose interlingual problems for learners whose equivalent L1 collocations have different phraseological characteristics. Such problems, however, need to be addressed explicitly for specified groups of learners. The following example does not seem to be justified by considerations of interference:

Table 5. Flower and Berman, 1989

Some pairs of words often occur together. If you see one of them, you can expect to see the other. This makes listening and reading easier! Here are some partnerships.

1. ask	a. a bicycle
2. climb	b. a boat
3. drink	c. a car
4. drive	d. a cigarette
5. eat	e. a cup of coffee
6. fly	f. a mountain
7. light	g. a plane
8. ride	h. a question
9. sail	i. a sandwich
10. tell	j. a story

[Flower and Berman 1989: 36]

A further example shows a similar lack of discrimination between what is phraseologically significant and what is rule-governed:

> **4** *He was a pleasant old fellow who always had something intelligent to say, and delighted everyone with his flow of___________ remarks.*
> **a)** *facetious* **b)** *vindictive* **c)** *witty* **d)** *ridiculous*
> [Lacey et al., 1990]

Any problems learners might face in acquiring the combination *witty remarks* are non-phraseological.

Of more value is the following type of exercise, in which learners are made aware of a choice between equivalent free and restricted expressions and the stylistic preference that native speakers might have for the more restricted alternative:

> Our university *gave* the mayor *an honorary degree.* [*award a degree*]
> We will *have the conference* in Tokyo. [*hold a conference*]
> [Benson et al., 1991]
>
> 1.*Security is very* __ *at that prison; there have been no less than four escapes this year.* (don't use: *bad, poor*). [*lax security*]
> 2.*Security is very* ___ *at the other prison. There has never been a successful escape from there.* (don't use: *good*) [*tight security*]
> 3.*How the newspapers found out about the new defence plan I don't know. There must have been a security* ___ *at the Ministry.* (don't use: *problem*) [*security leak*]
> [McCarthy et al., 1985]

CONCLUSION

It is necessary to be cautious in making strong statements about learners' needs in this highly complex area of competence, and it would be wrong to raise anxiety by laying great emphasis on knowledge that is very difficult to describe and which native writers may have imperfect control of. Some attempts can be made, however, to raise awareness of features of writing that can have a serious impact on the effectiveness of communication, and there is certainly scope for great improvements in the design of teaching materials to achieve this. The key to this is an understanding of what is significant in phraseological units and a much sharper focus on aspects of restriction.

REFERENCES

Benson, M., Benson, E., Ilson, R. and Young, R. (1991) *Using the BBI.* Amsterdam and Philadelphia: John Benjamins.

Cop, M. (1988) The function of collocations in dictionaries. In T Magay and J Zigany (eds). *BUDALEX Proceedings*: Papers from the EURALEX Third International Congress. Budapest: Akademiai Kiado.

Dechert, H. and Lennon, P. (1989) Collocational blends of advanced language learners: a preliminary analysis. In W Olesky (ed) *Contrastive Pragmatics.* Amsterdam: John Benjamins.

Flower, J. and Berman, M. (1989) *Build Your Vocabulary.* Hove: Language Teaching Publications.

Howarth, P. (1993) A phraseological approach to academic writing. In G Blue (ed.) *Language, Learning and Success: Studying through English.* London: Macmillan.

Johansson, S. (1977) Problems in studying the communicative effect of learners' errors. In A Valdman (ed) *Studies in Second Language Acquisition.* Vol 1. Bloomington: The Indiana University Linguistics Club.

Korosadowicz-Struyñska, M. (1980) Word combinations in FL vocabulary instruction. *Studia Anglia Posnaniensia* 12:109-120.

Lacey, C., Mahood, J., Trench, J. and Vanderpump, E. (1990) *Increase your Vocabulary.* Oxford: Oxford University Press.
McCarthy, M., Maclean, A. and O'Malley, P. (1985) *Proficiency Plus.* Oxford: Blackwell.
Pawley, A. and Syder, F.H. (1983) Two puzzles for linguistic theory: nativelike selection and nativelike fluency. In JC Richards and RW Schmidt (eds) *Language and Communication.* London: Longman.
Sinclair, J. (1991) *Corpus, Concordance, Collocation.* Oxford: Oxford University Press.

Notes on contributors

Alasdair Archibald is a lecturer in EAP at the School of Modern Languages, University of Southampton. His interests are in discourse analysis, second language writing, and error analysis and interlanguage theories.

Richard Badger lectures in the Centre for English Language Teaching, the University of Stirling. His research interests include ESP, legal discourse, teaching writing as genre, and testing.

George Blue teaches EAP and Applied Linguistics at the University of Southampton. His interests include learner autonomy, self-assessment, individual learner differences, language in education and various aspects of EAP.

Hilary Bool is the Director of The Centre for English Language Education, University of Nottingham. Her career has spanned teaching in secondary schools both in the UK and overseas, delivering ESP courses in aviation/military contexts, teacher development programmes and EAP. Research interests focus on cultural issues within language teaching.

Jane Clarke is a researcher at the Department of Adult Education, Leicester University, working on widening provision for adults from minority ethnic communities. She has taught ESOL in Britain and abroad, and now teaches Mass Media and Popular Culture in the department.

Paul Fanning has taught English for Academic Purposes since he became lecturer at Middlesex University in 1986. He currently specialises in in-sessional EAP and EFL teacher training.

Ann Gavriel has been English Language Tutor at the Robert Gordon University in Aberdeen since 1993. Her TESOL activities began in 1967 while working in Iran as a trainee sub-editor. She began designing and teaching ESP programmes in 1986 and has believed ever since that all language teaching is 'for specific purposes'.

Katie Gray is the Director for Language Studies at Oxford University Department for Continuing Education. Her recent publications have focused on syllabus design, language awareness and the cultural aspects of teaching and learning. She is the editor of the *Japanese Learner*.

Roxy Harris is a Senior Lecturer in the School of English Language Education and its associated Centre for Applied Linguistic Research at Thames Valley University. He is interested in the factors affecting the acquisition of academic literacies.

Brenda P. Imber teaches oral discourse and writing at the University of Michigan's English Language Institute; coordinates and teaches ELI's ITA and the international pre-MBA course, and is co-author of *Integrated Lessons: Pronunciation and Grammar.*

Jiawei Liu is a technical translator at System Software Associates in Chicago. She is a part-time student at CELTE, University of Warwick, and has just completed a doctorate on technical and sub-technical vocabulary.

Alan Lockett works at the Language Centre, University of Bristol, where lectures on and co-ordinates the pre-sessional and in-sessional English programmes. His interests are in discourse/genre analysis and academic writing.

Philip Luford has taught EAP in Australia and Britain and has also taught in the field of science and technology studies. He works at the Centre for English Language Education, University of Nottingham. His interests are in the politics of English as a world language.

Damien McDevitt works as an adviser for INSET in Botswana. He previously lectured for the Centre for English Language Teaching, University of Stirling. His interests are staff development, Inservice work, and language policies.

Ann Montemayor-Borsinger is a lecturer of English at Instituto Balseiro, Universidad Nacional de Cuyo in Argentina and is currently doing a PhD in Linguistics at the University of Glasgow. She has worked as a teacher in Europe and Latin America. Her interests focus on academic writing in the sciences.

Catherine Montgomery is a teaching fellow at the University of Essex. Her teaching and research interests are in the field of EAP and ESP. She is particularly interested in issues surrounding the assessment of student writing.

Hilary Nesi is a lecturer at CELTE, University of Warwick. Her research interests include EAP, learner dictionary design, and CALL. She has contributed to journals and books in these areas.

Maria G. Parker teaches writing and oral discourse at the University of Michigan's English Language Institute, conducts research in ELI's testing division, coordinates ELI's pre-MBA English for Business Studies Course, and is co-author of *Integrated Lessons: Pronunciation and Grammar.*

Linda Pearsall is a teaching fellow at the University of Essex. She has taught extensively on a range of EAP courses and has research interests in EAP, teacher training, and teaching English to young learners.

Carol Saunders is the Director of Learning Development at De Montfort University. Her interest in student writing emerged from her experience as a cultural studies lecturer. Apart from publications on subject discourse and modularity, she has co-authored books for students on transferable skills and published articles on postmodern consumption patterns.

Barbara Thornton has worked in Cyprus, Finland, Germany and the Middle East and is currently teaching at Leicester University. Her interests lie in the areas of teacher education and she is currently doing a Ph.D. in the area of language anxiety.

Dilys Thorp was until recently senior lecturer at Thames Valley University. In addition to teaching EAP she has worked on teacher education courses, and was responsible for the MA in ELT module on materials development for ESP and general purpose contexts. She now works as a freelance consultant/trainer.

Joan Turner is head of the English Language Unit at Goldsmith's College, University of London. In both teaching and research she focuses on the relationship between language use and cultural values in academic discourse.

Sue Vincent taught EAP for 3 years at Warsaw University and then at Middlesex from 1991 where she maintained an interest in the ESP needs of Eastern Europe as well as developing new Business courses for students from France. She eventually supervised a new modular degree course entitled English for Business Communication. She retired through ill health in 1997 and, sadly, passed away in the December of that year.